MY FIRST EASTER

HIGH CONTRAST BABY BOOK

THIS BOOK BELONGS TO:

_____

_____

Happy Easter

GUIDANCES

HOW OFTEN SHOULD YOU VIEW THE BOOKS?

DO IT EVERY DAY. SHOW YOUR CHILD FOR AT LEAST A FEW MINUTES EVERY DAY. "WATCH AS MUCH AS YOU CAN."

HOW LONG SHOULD BABIES LOOK AT BLACK AND WHITE CARDS?

LET YOUR CHILD FOCUS ON THE PICTURE FOR A SHORT TIME, NO LONGER THAN 30 SECONDS AT A TIME.

MOTOR DEVELOPMENT - HAND-EYE?

ENCOURAGE YOUR BABY TO REACH FOR THE CARD AND EXAMINE IT WITH THEIR HANDS.

HO-HO-HO!
ENJOY THE GIFT INSIDE

https://bit.ly/*********

THE GIFT IN PAGE 26

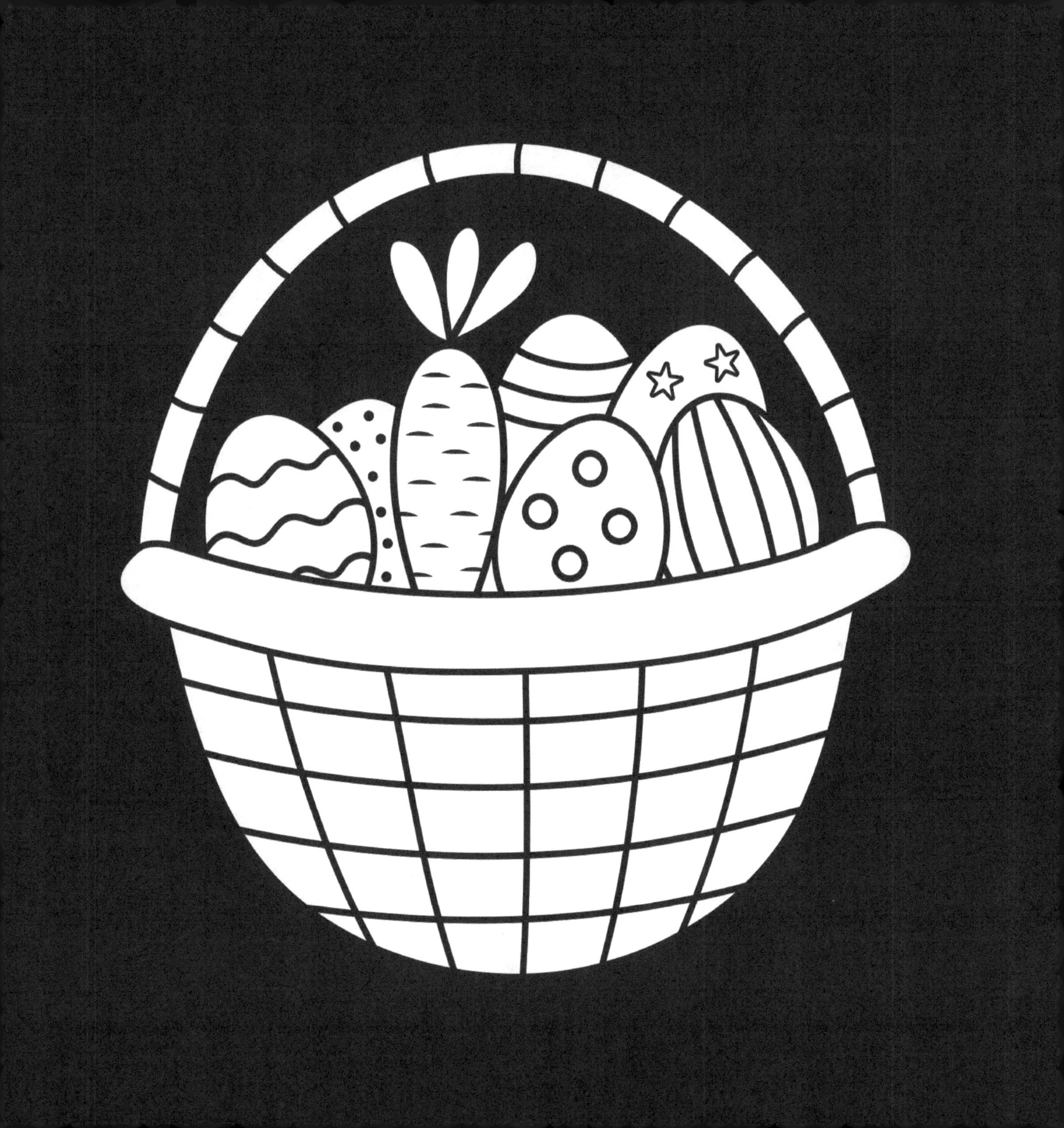

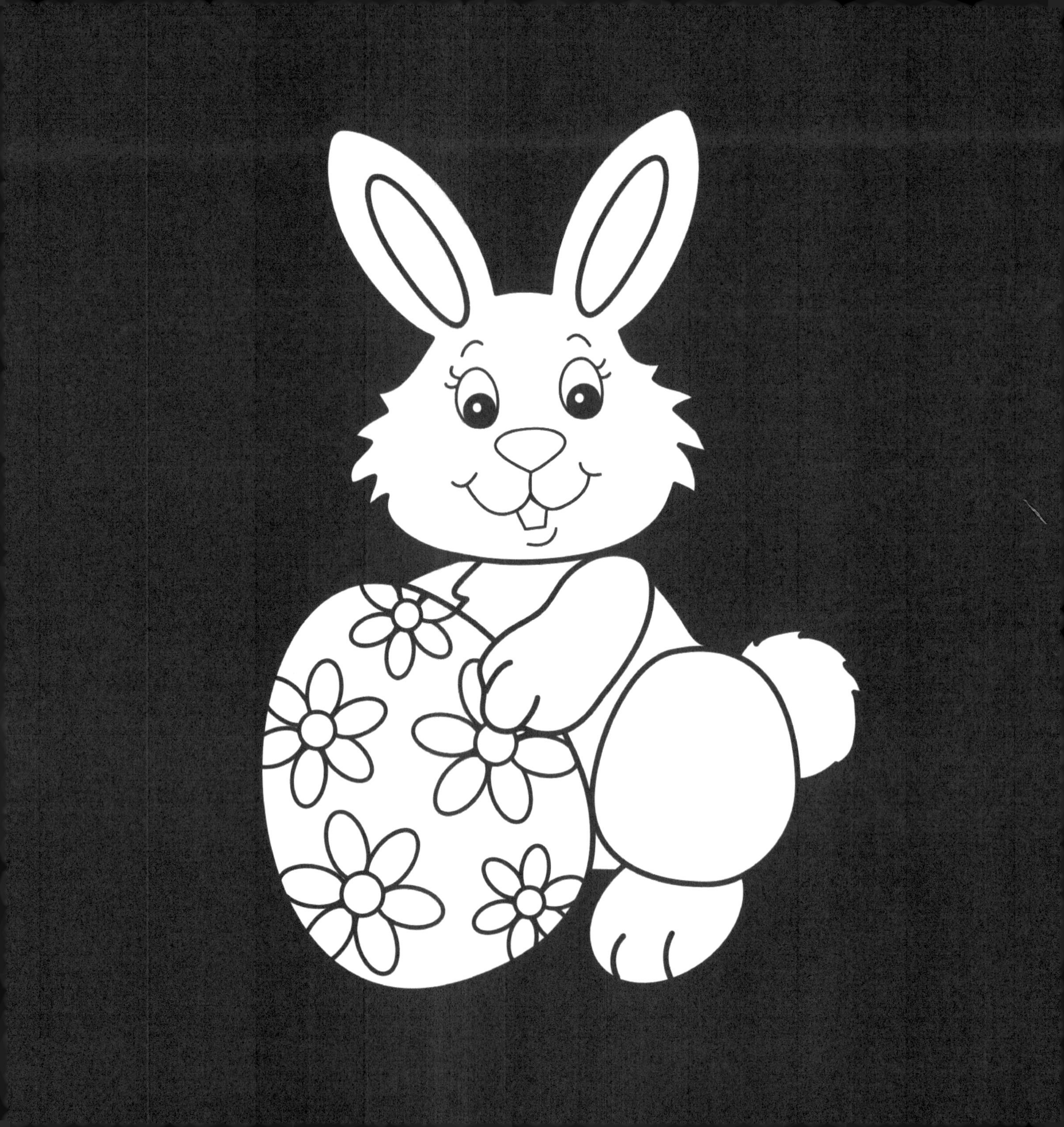

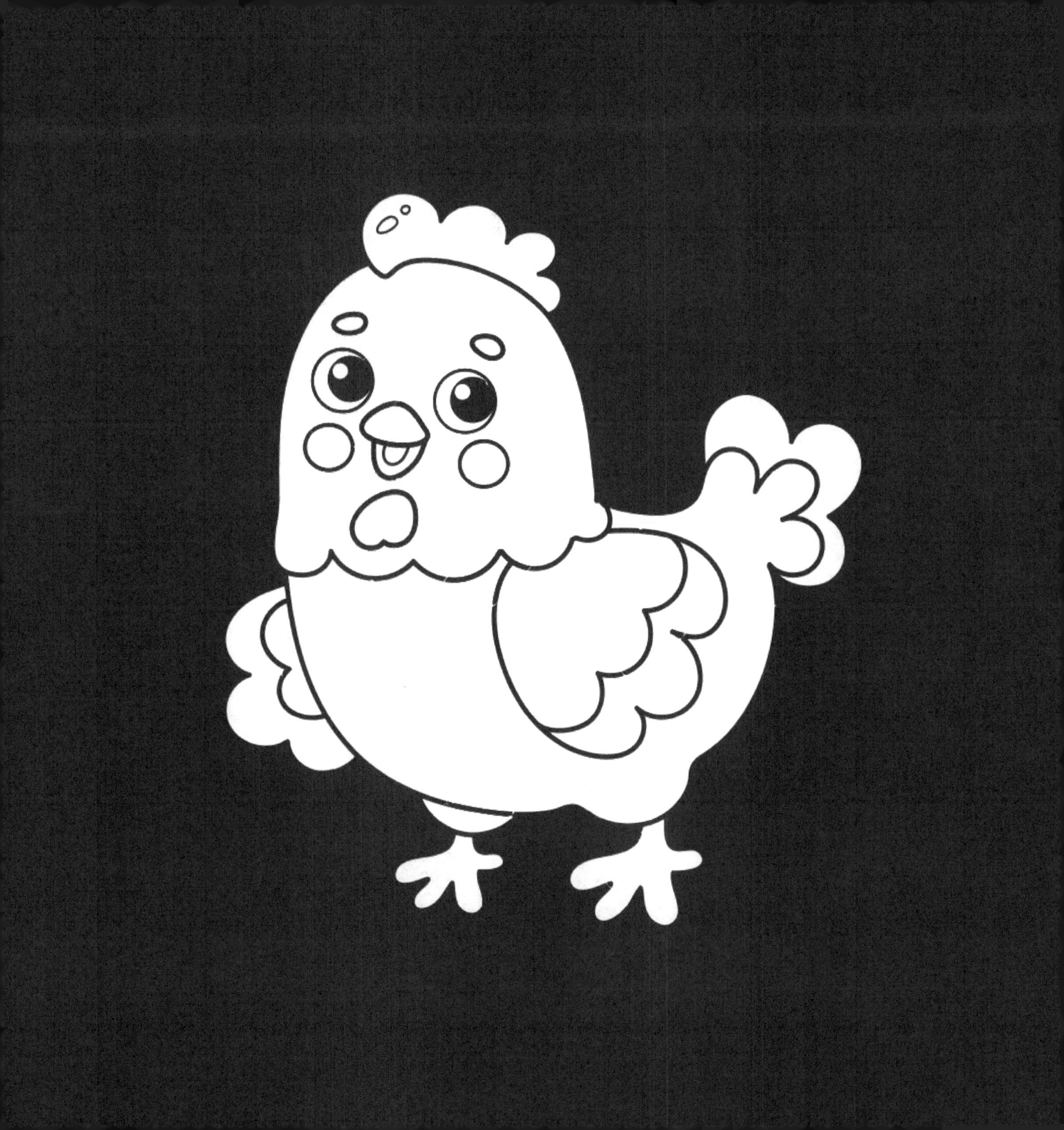

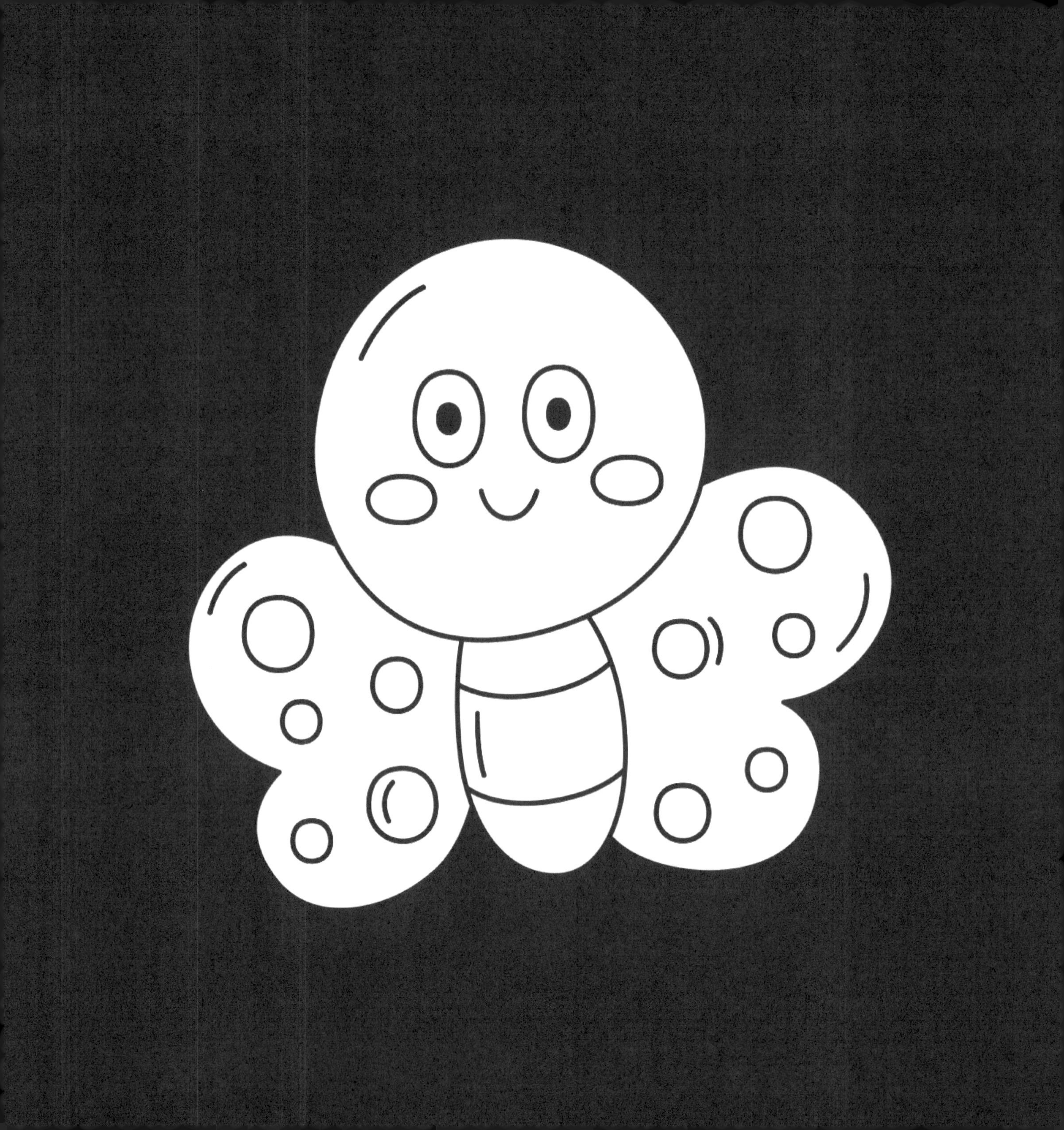

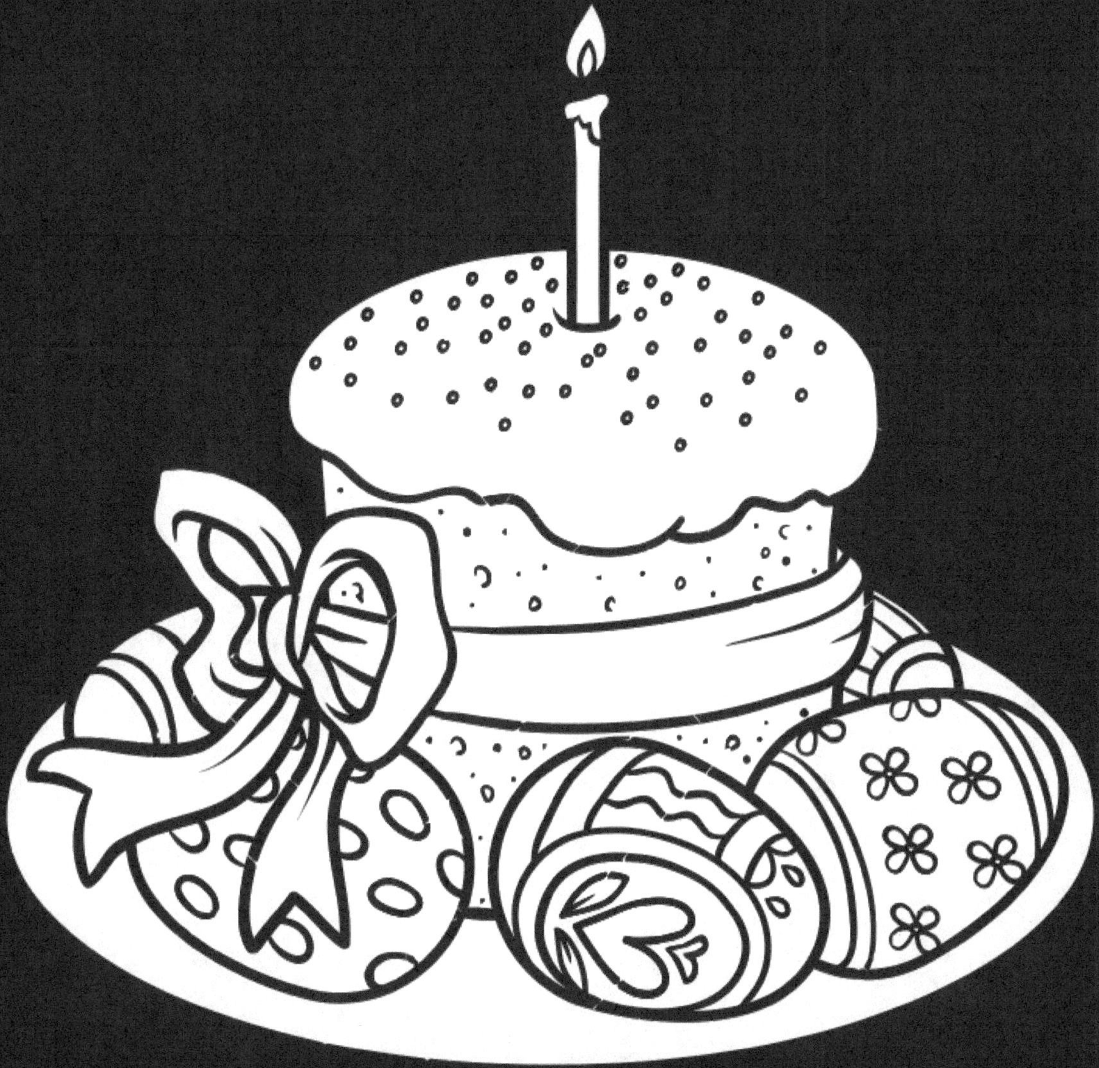

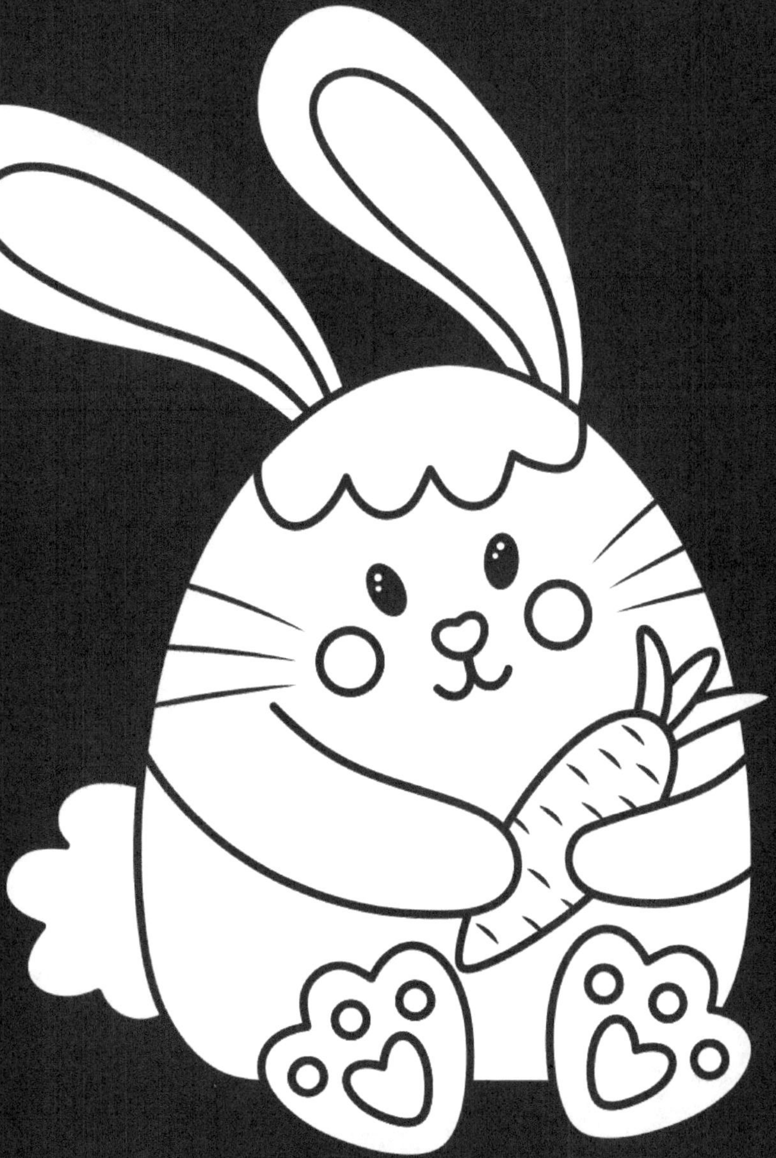

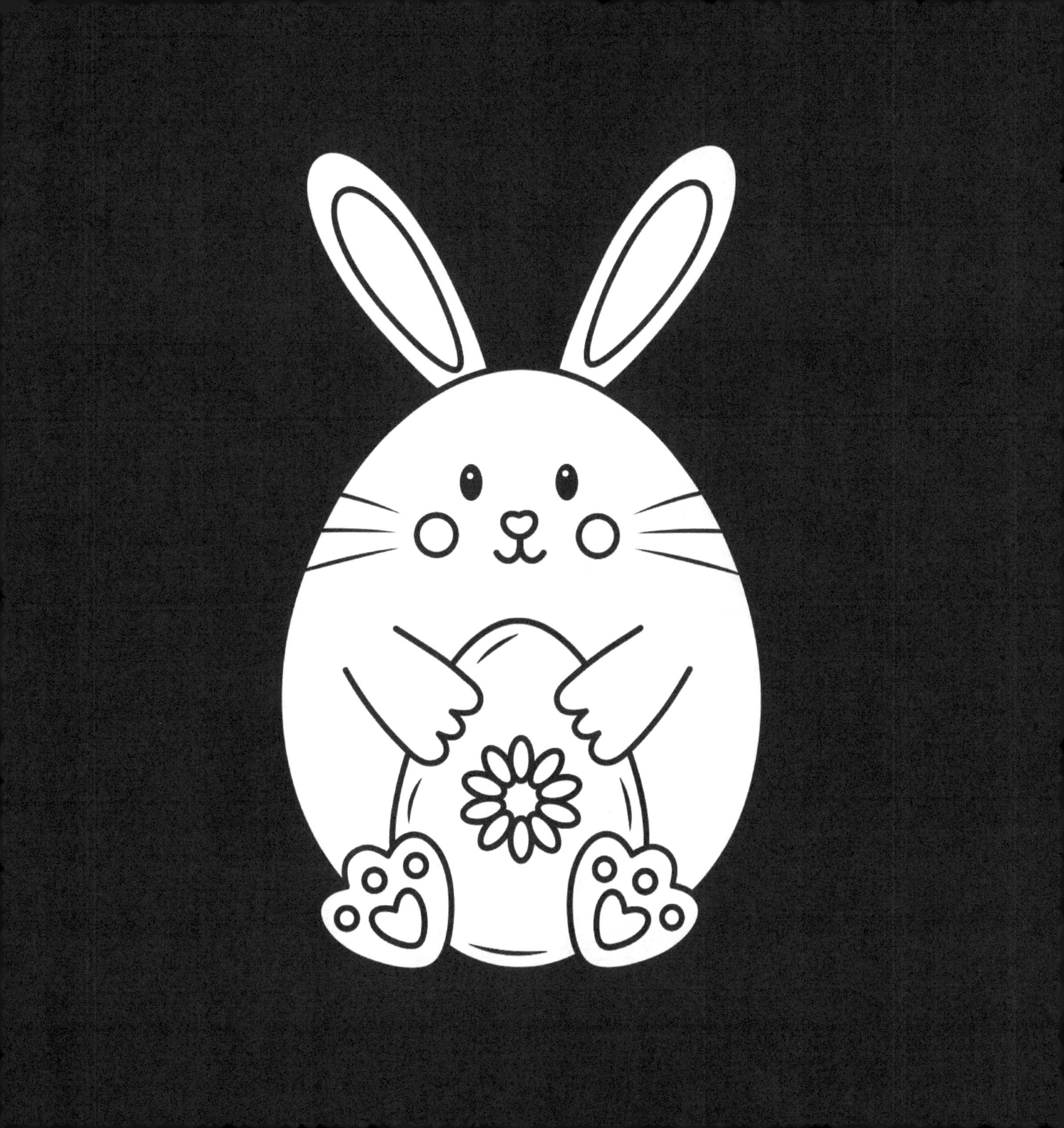

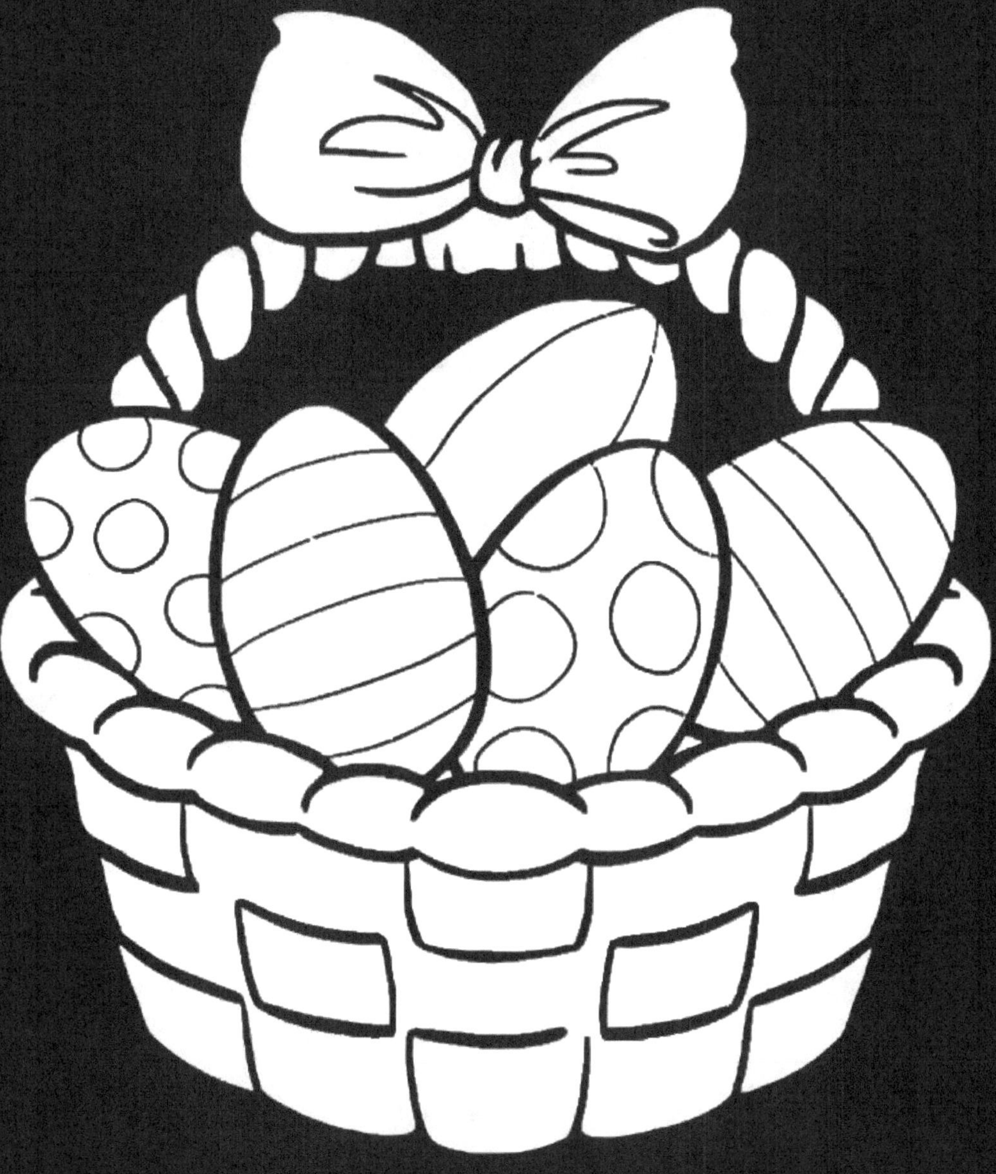

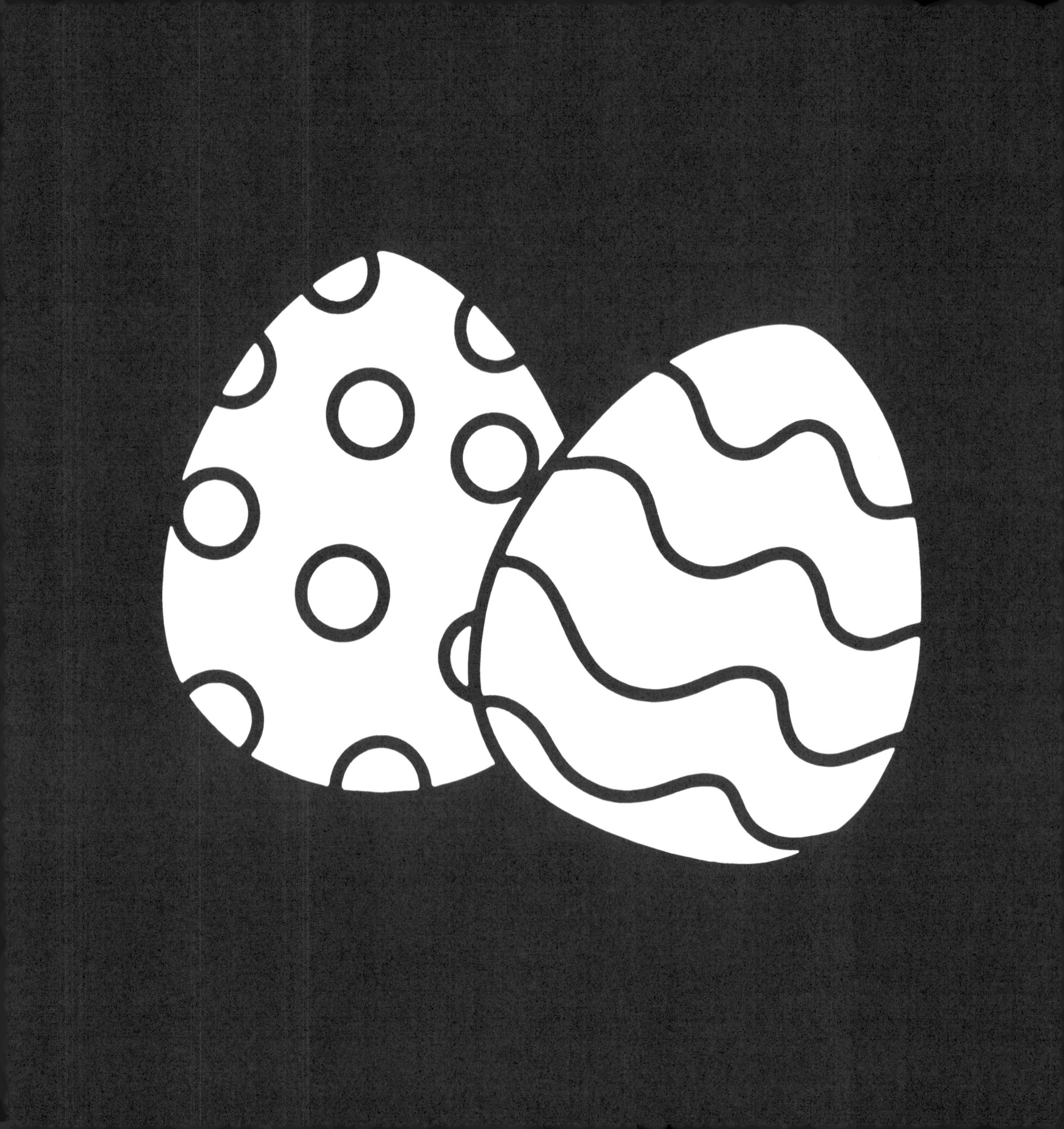

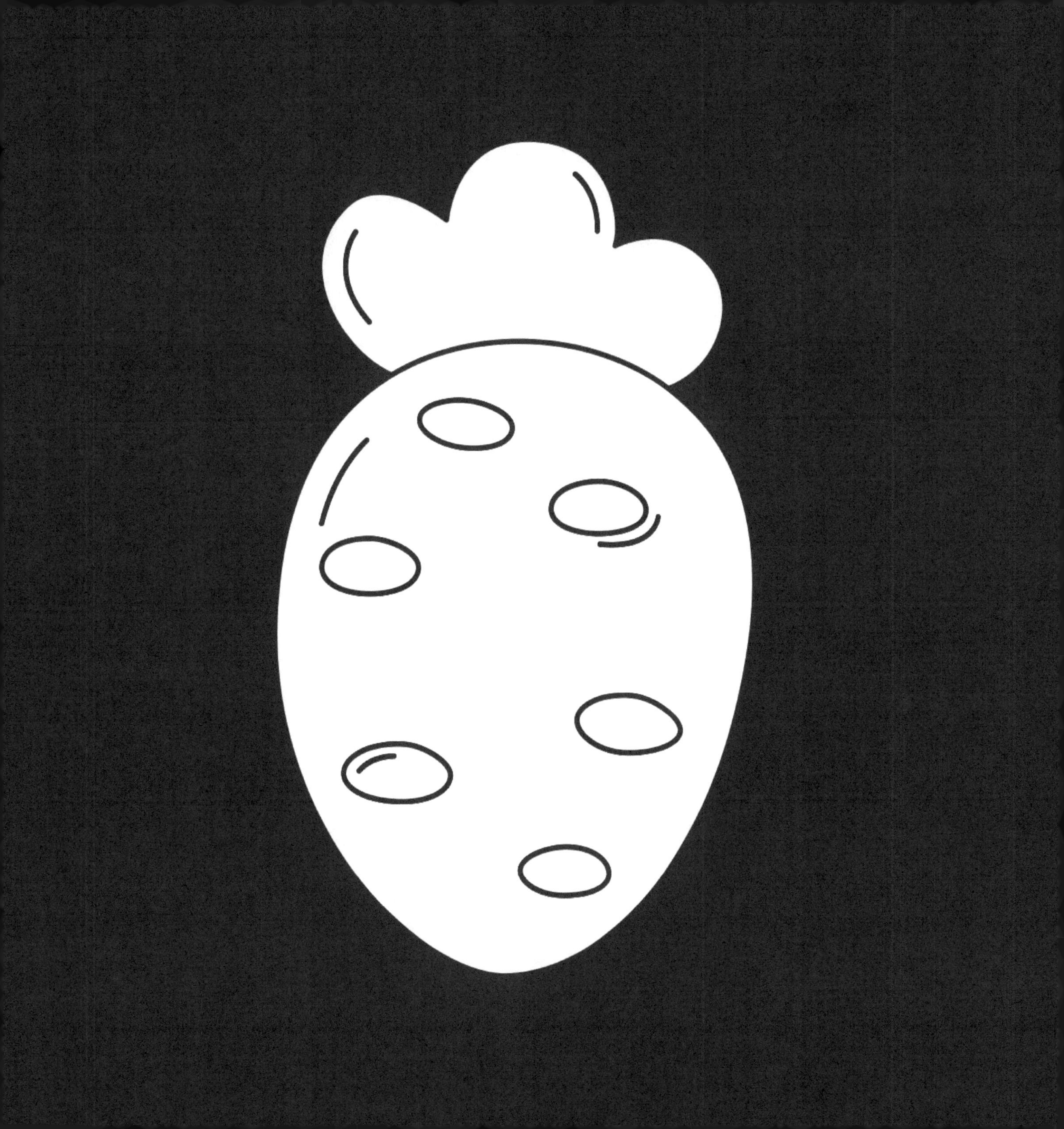

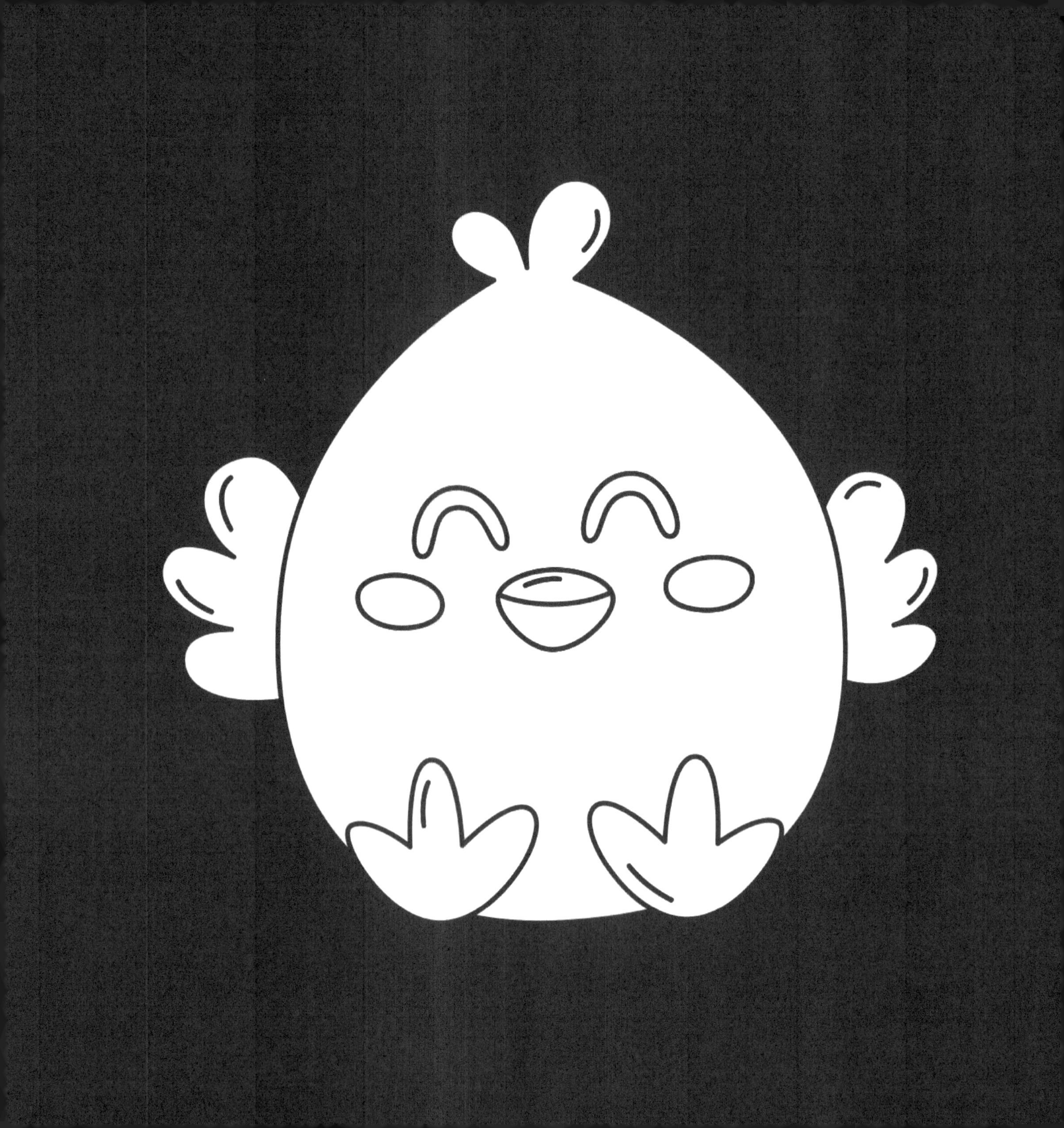

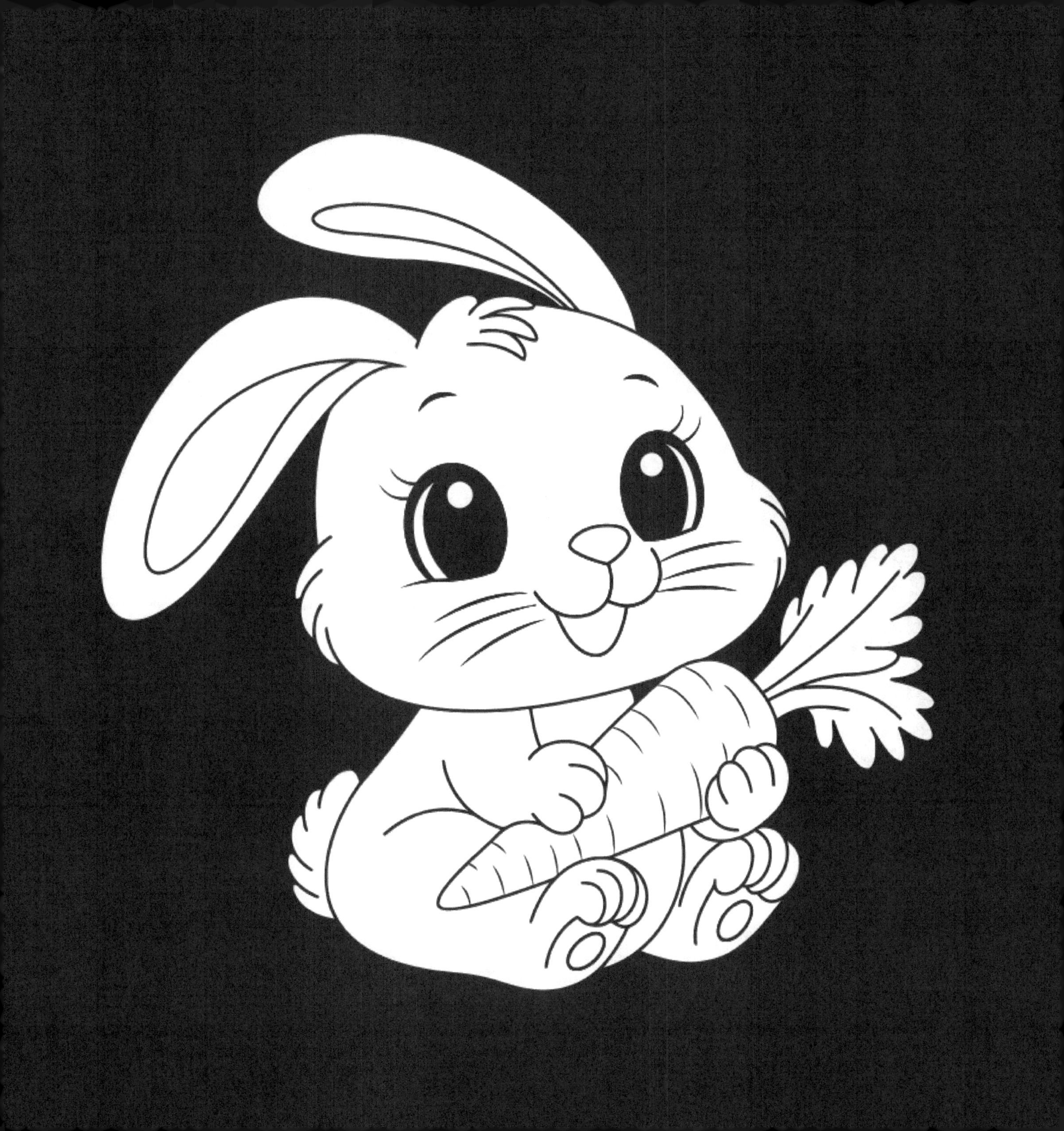

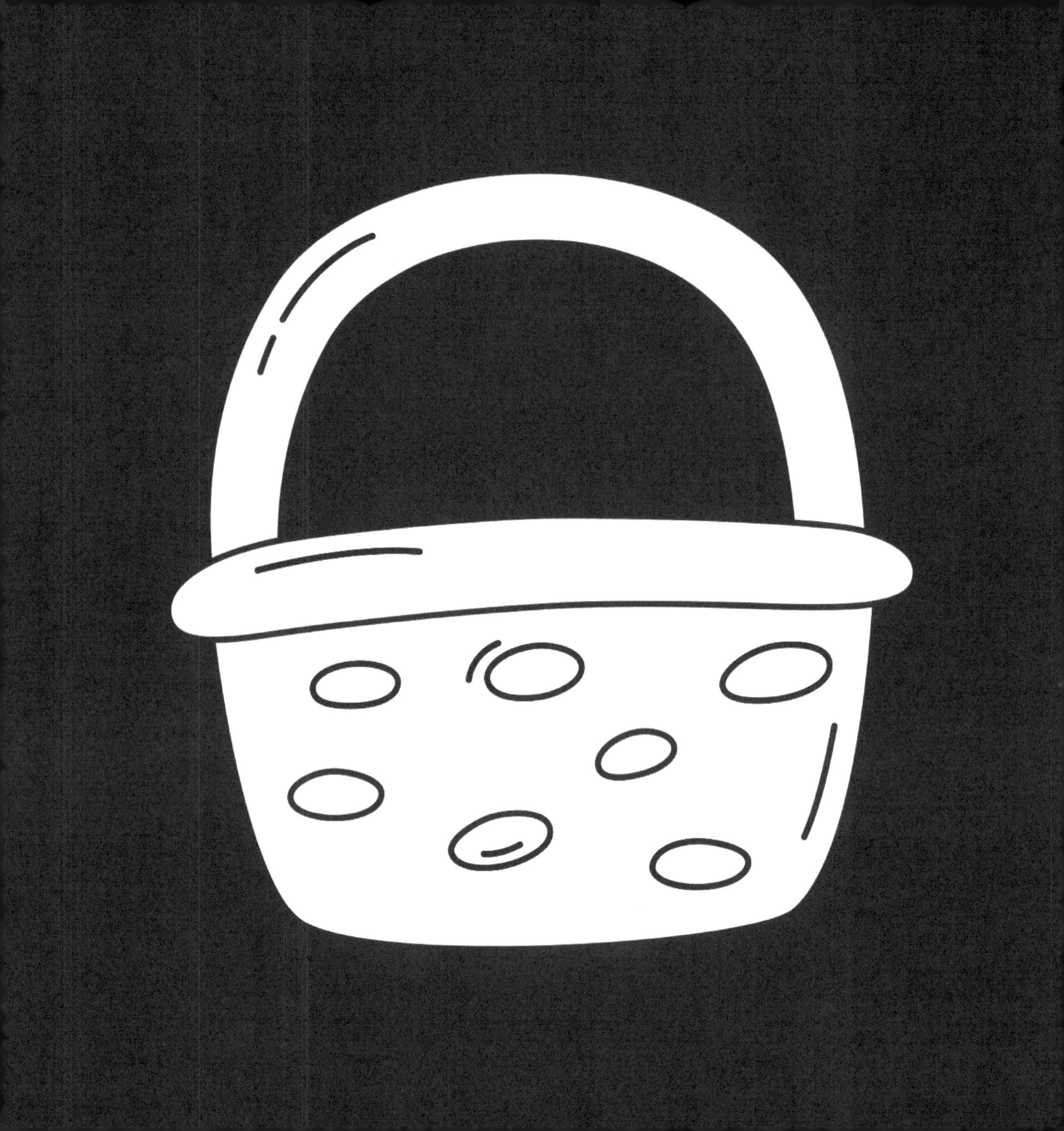

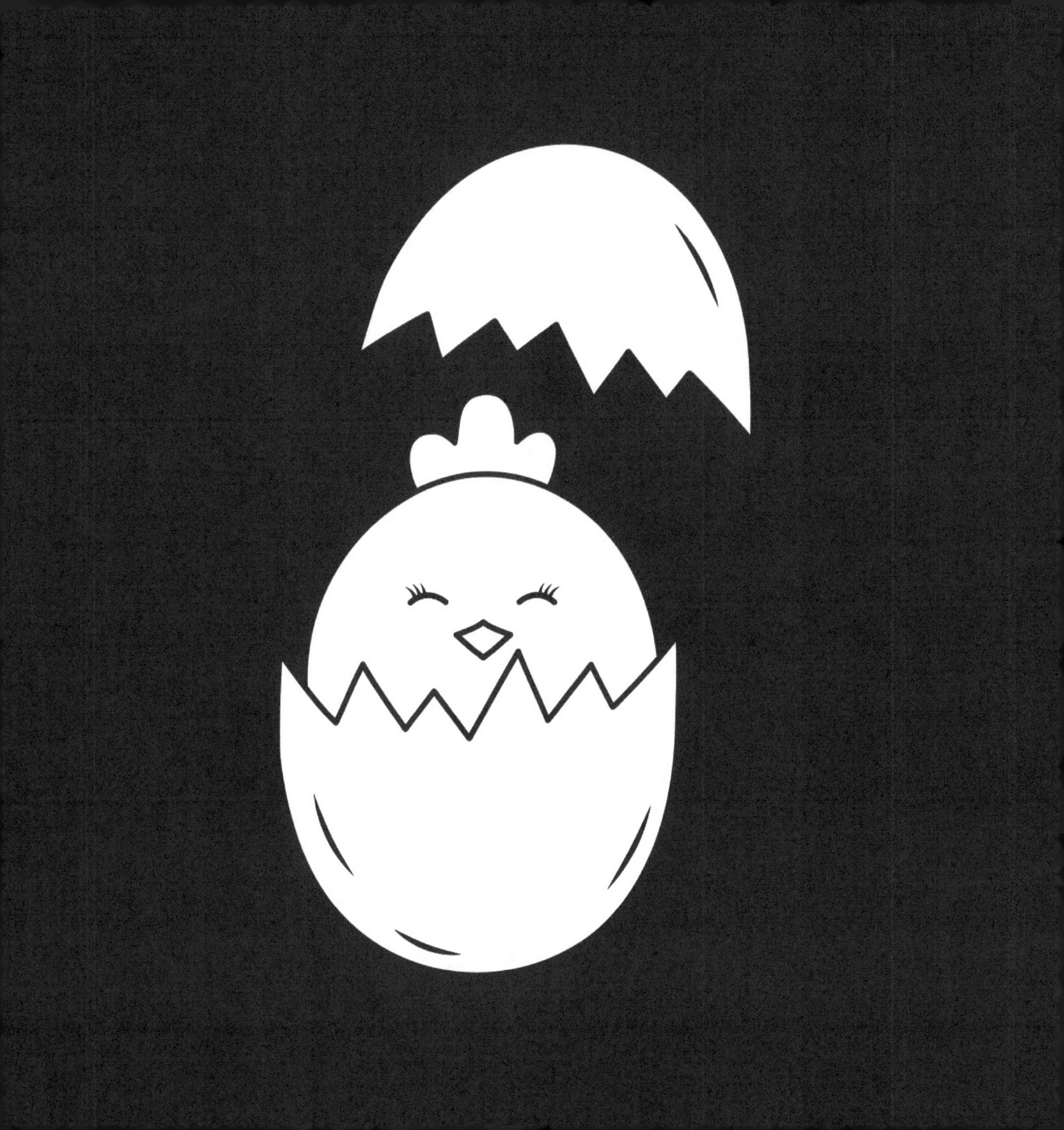

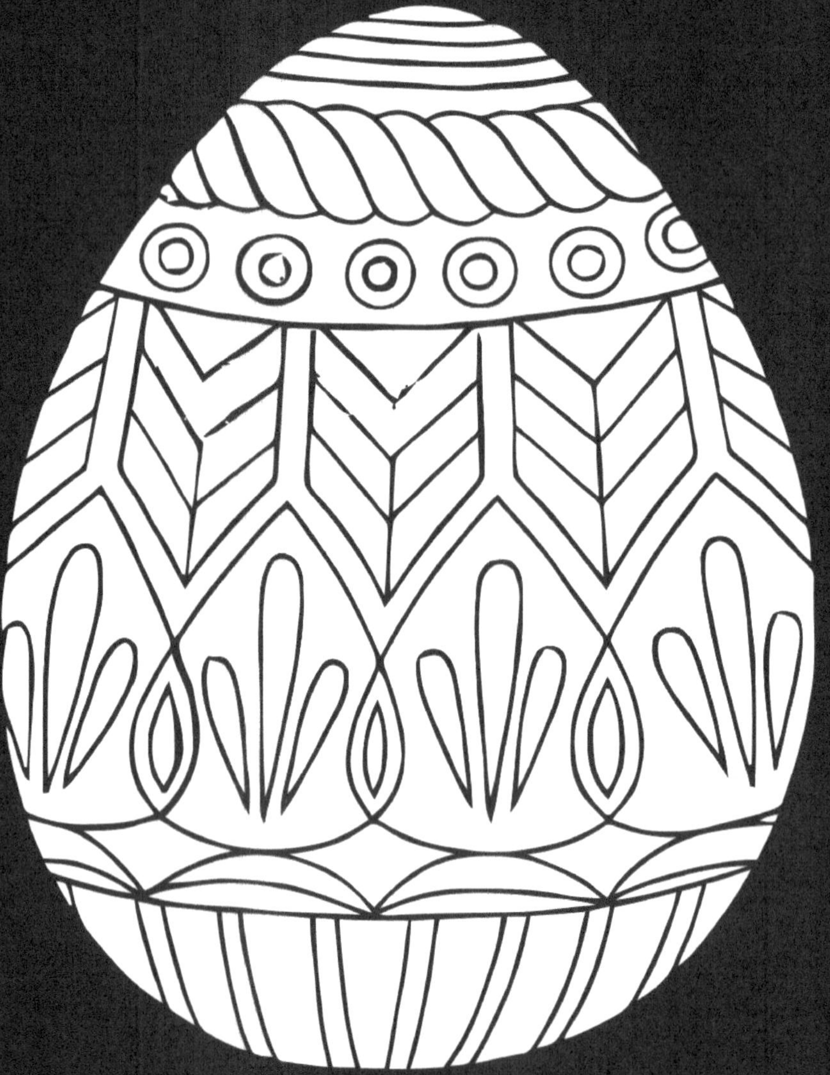

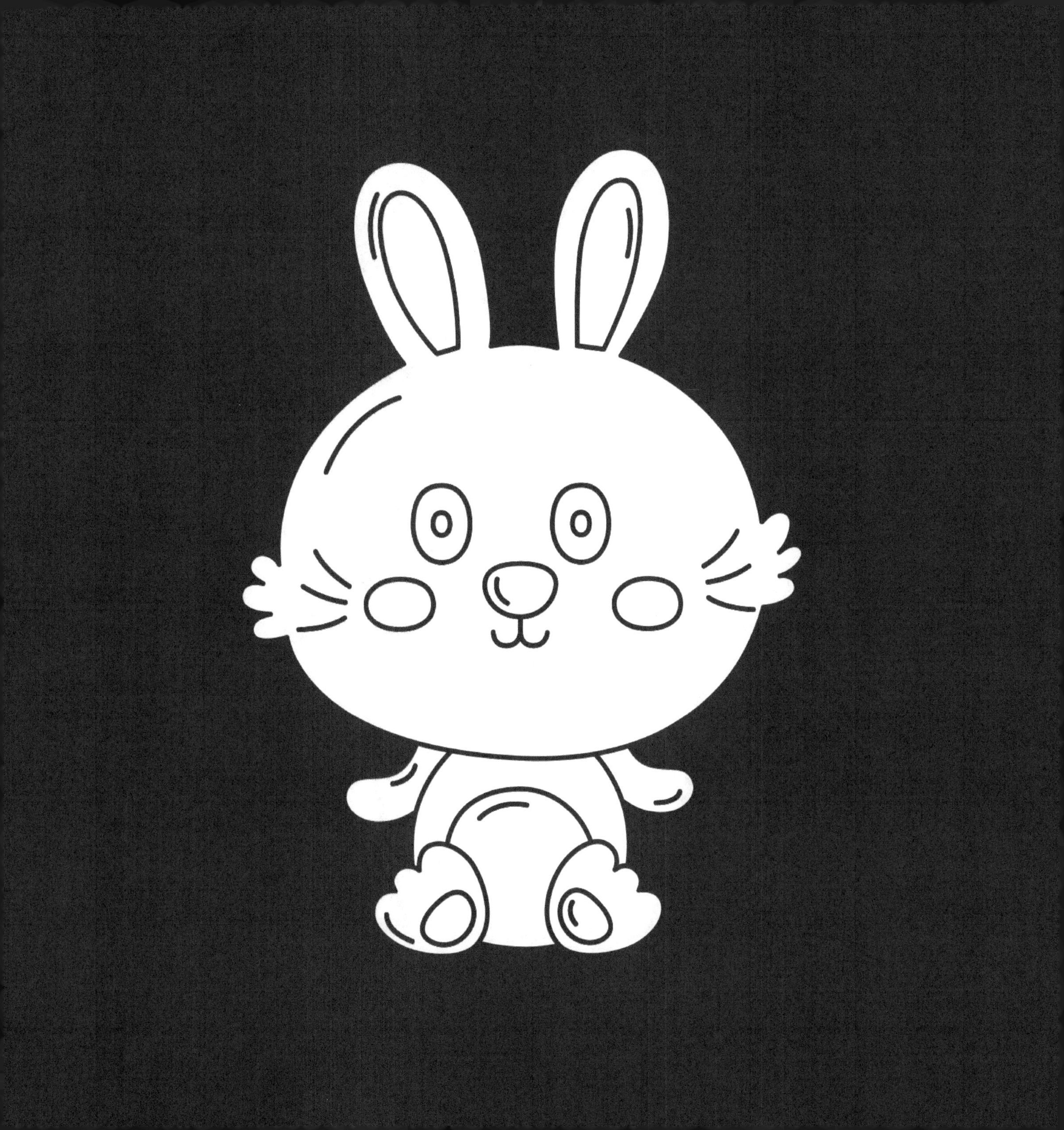

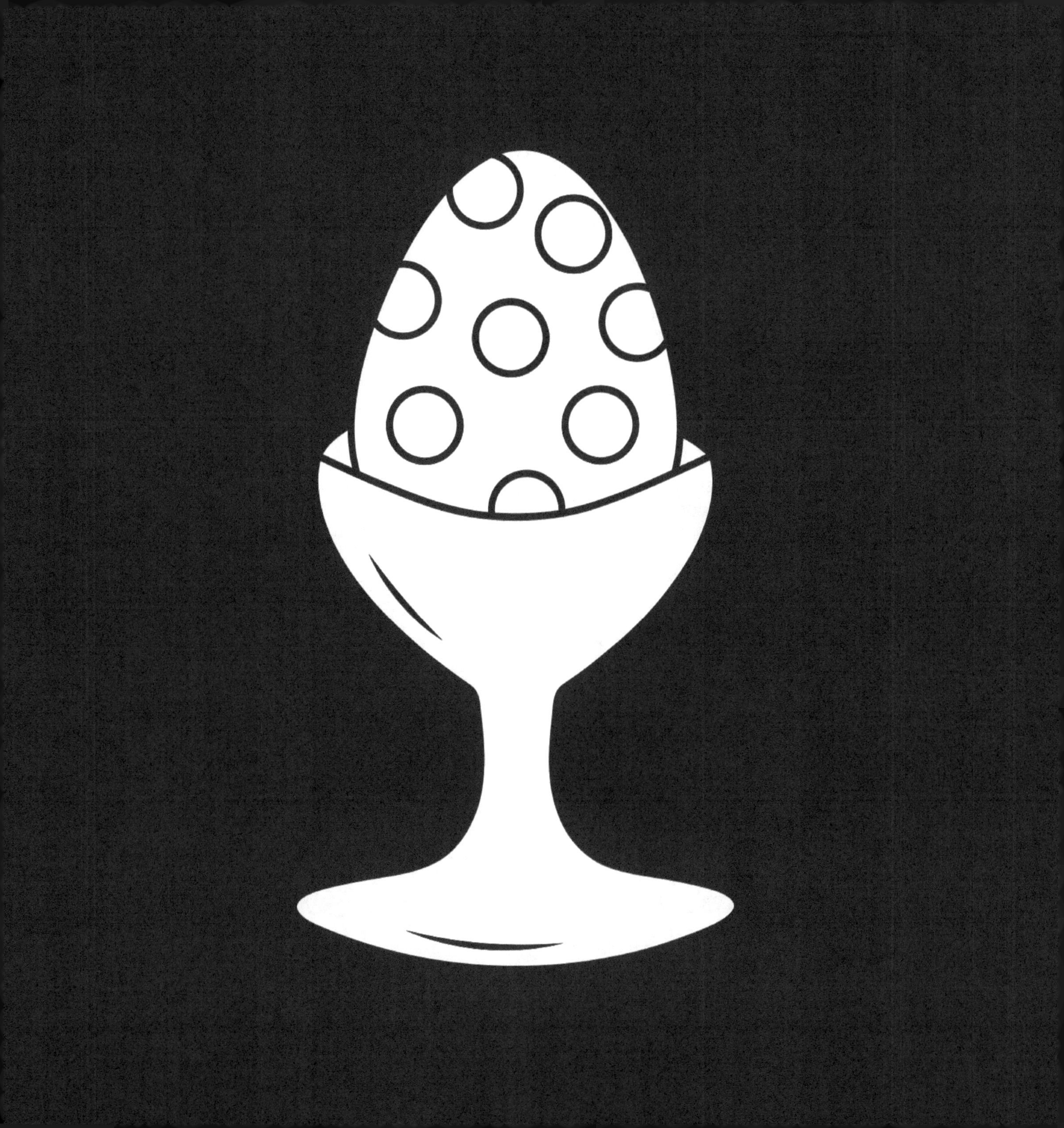

HO-HO-HO!

HERE IS YOUR GIFT:

https://bit.ly/4f4YOoW

TAP THIS LINK IN THE BROWSER AND ENJOY! IF YOU LOVED THE BOOK AND THE GIFT GIVE US

★★★★★

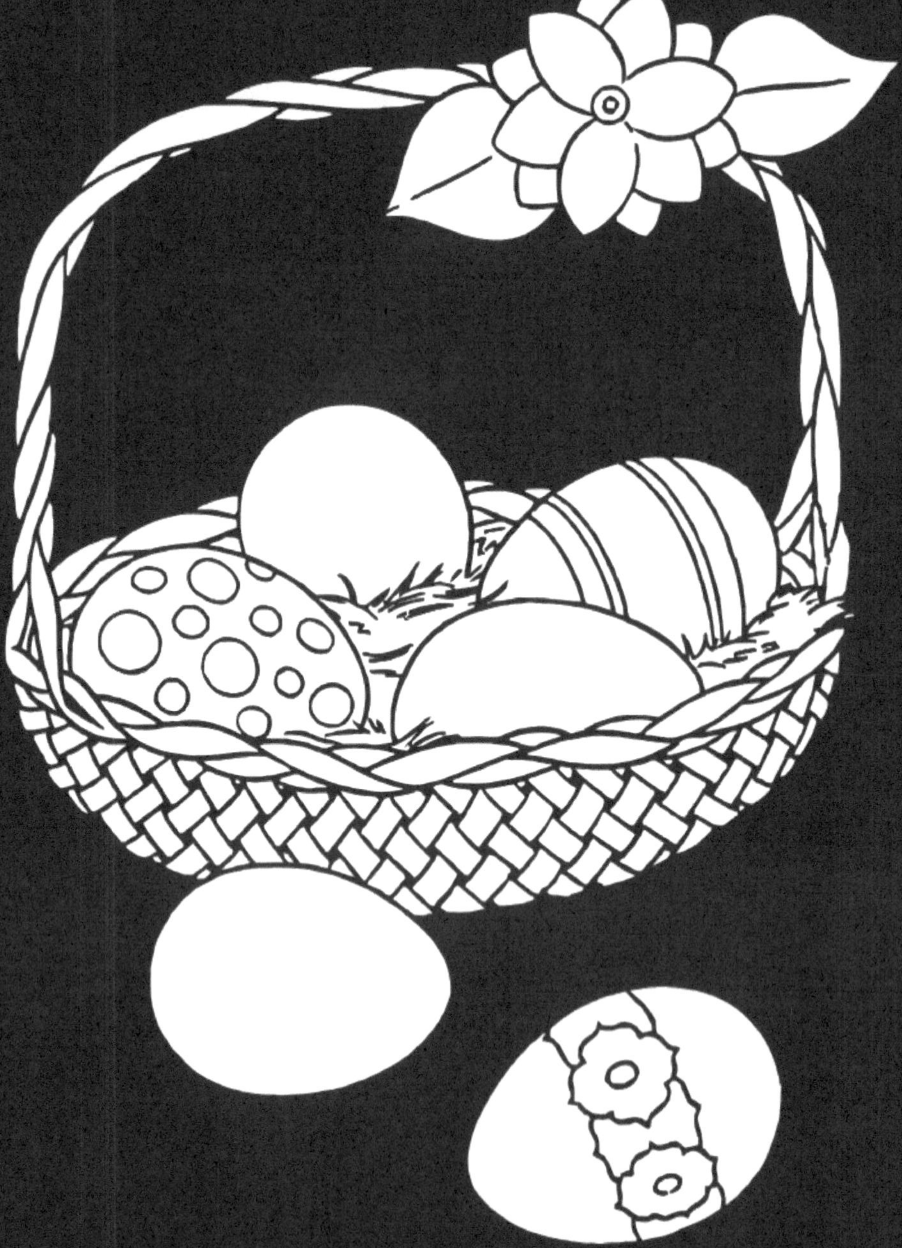

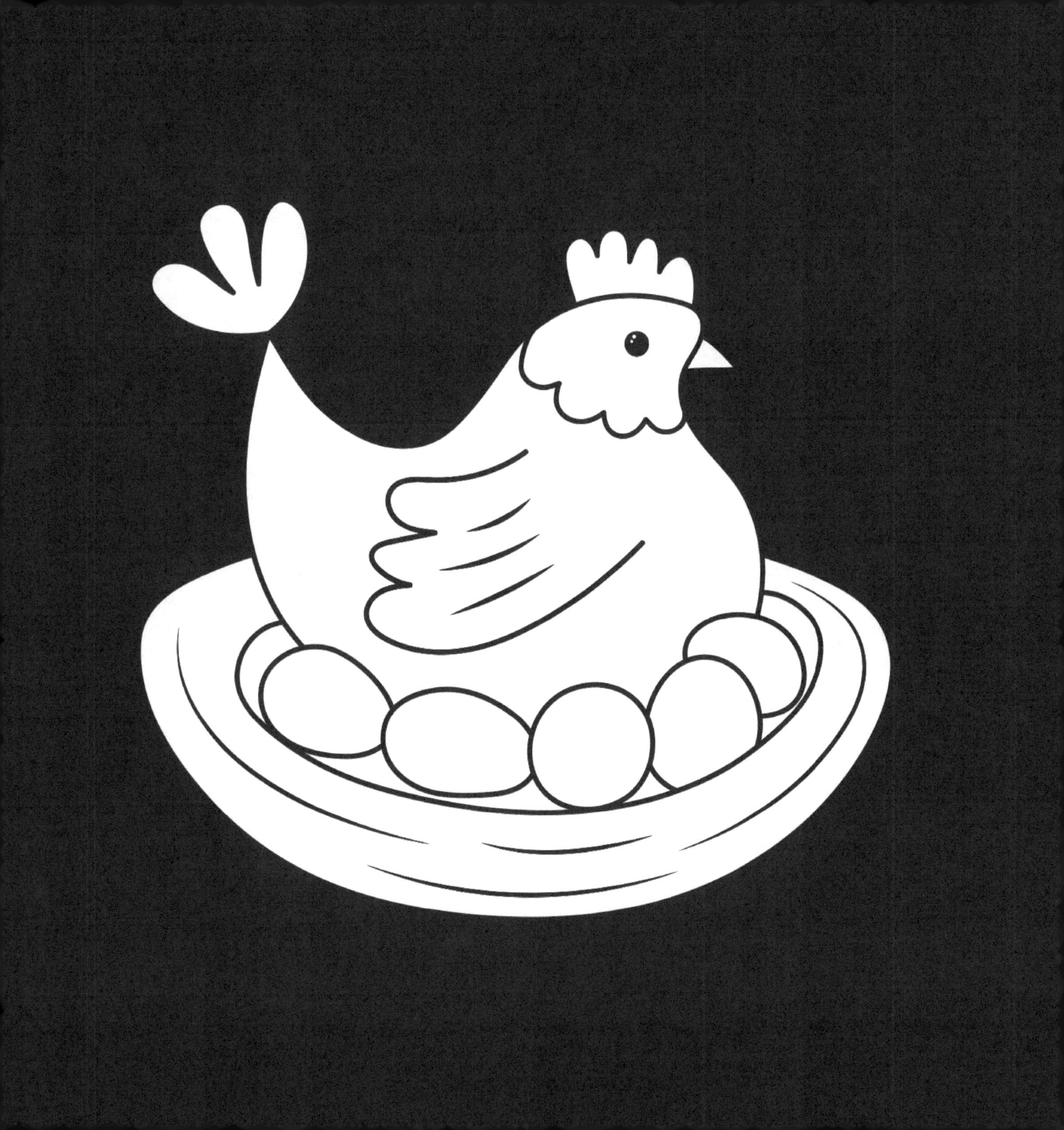

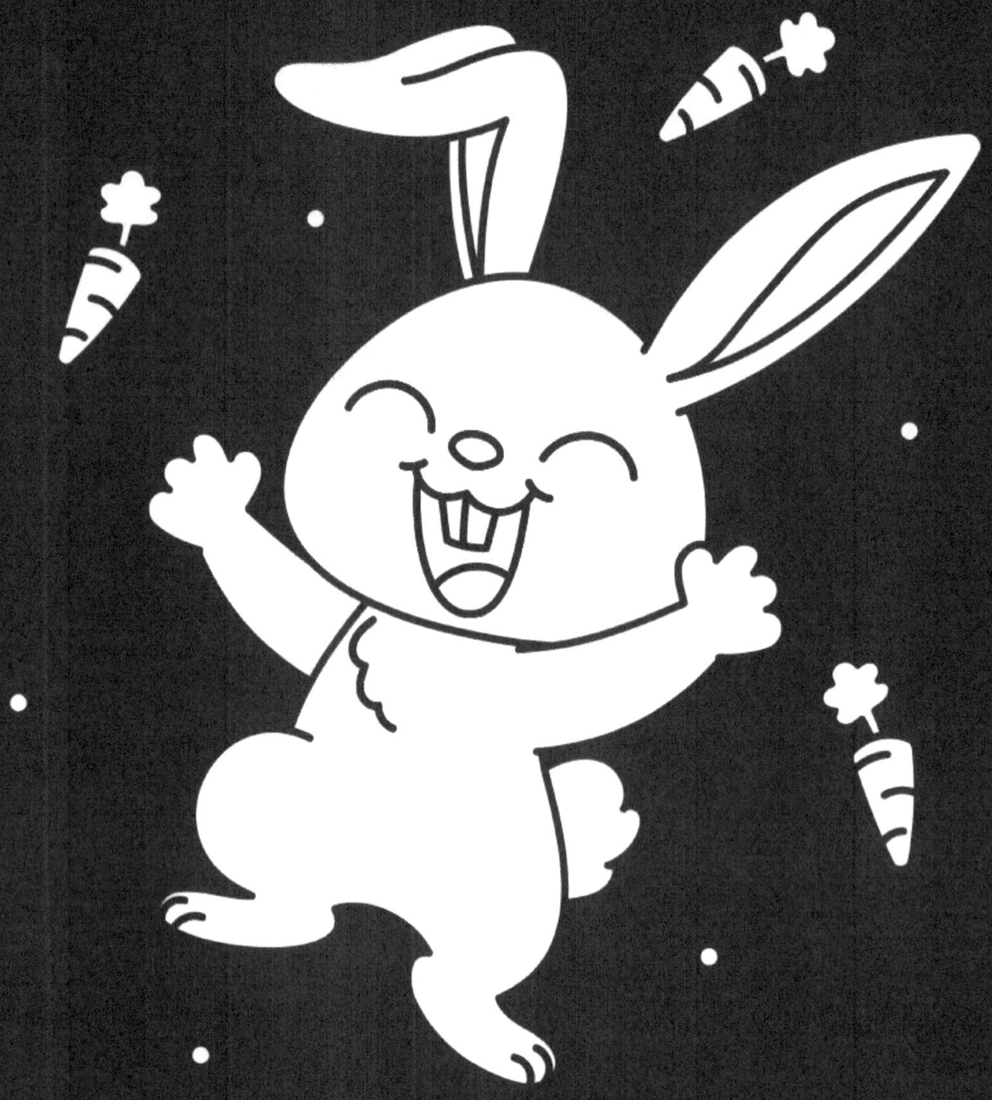

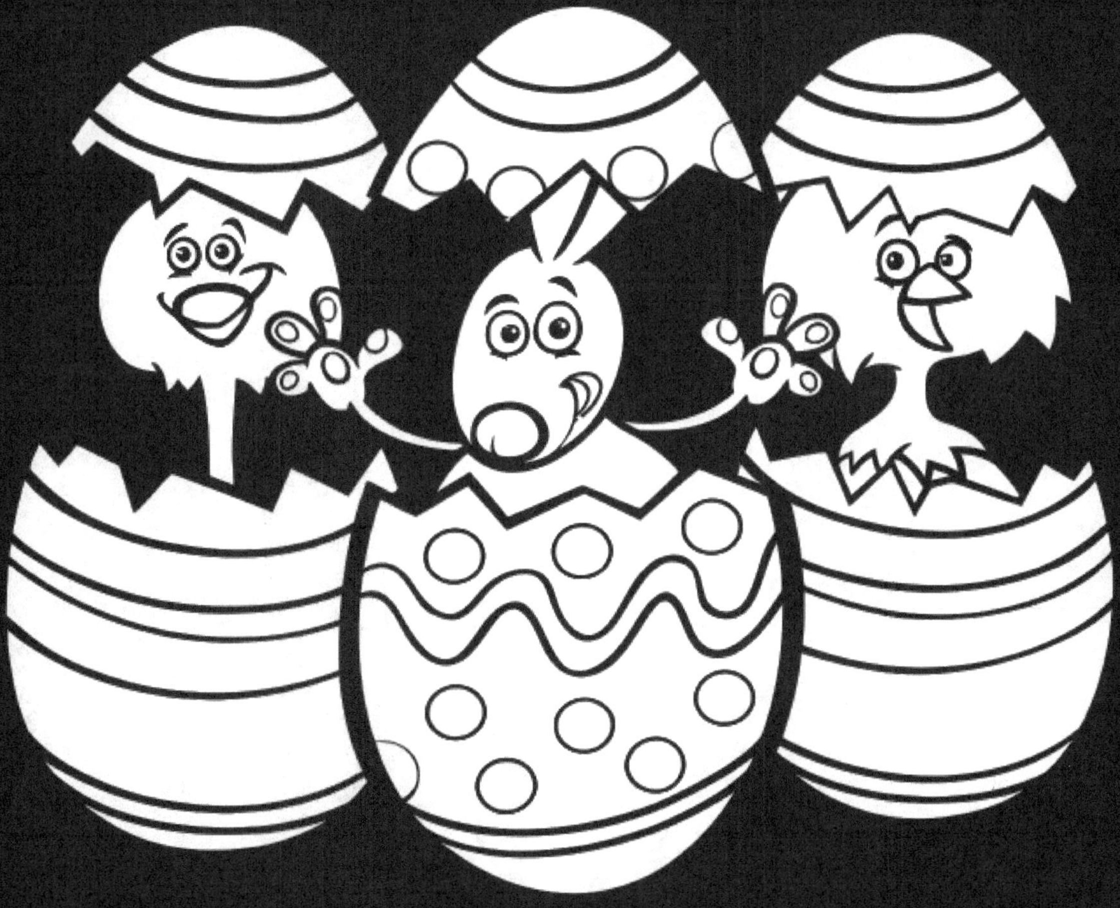

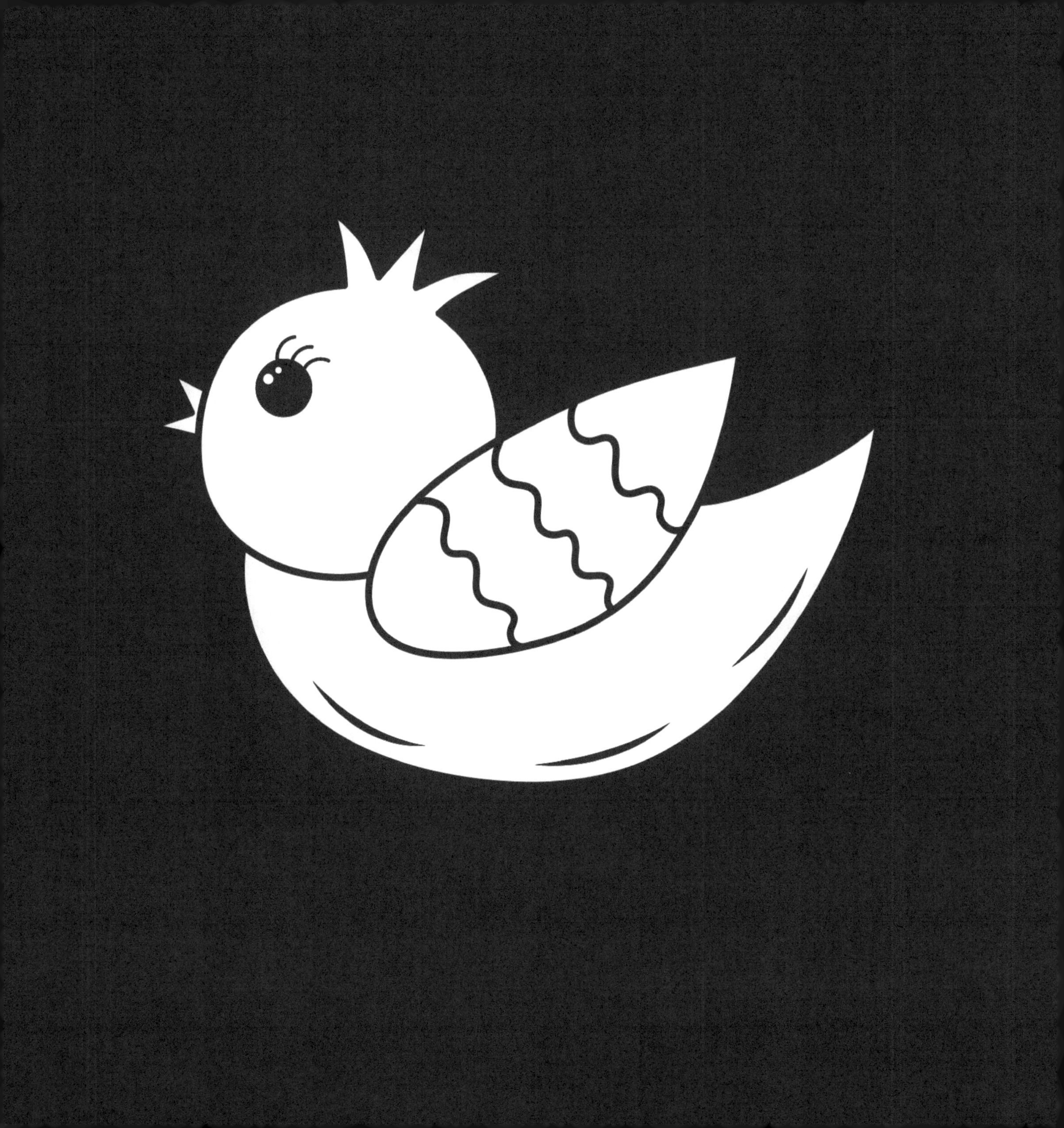

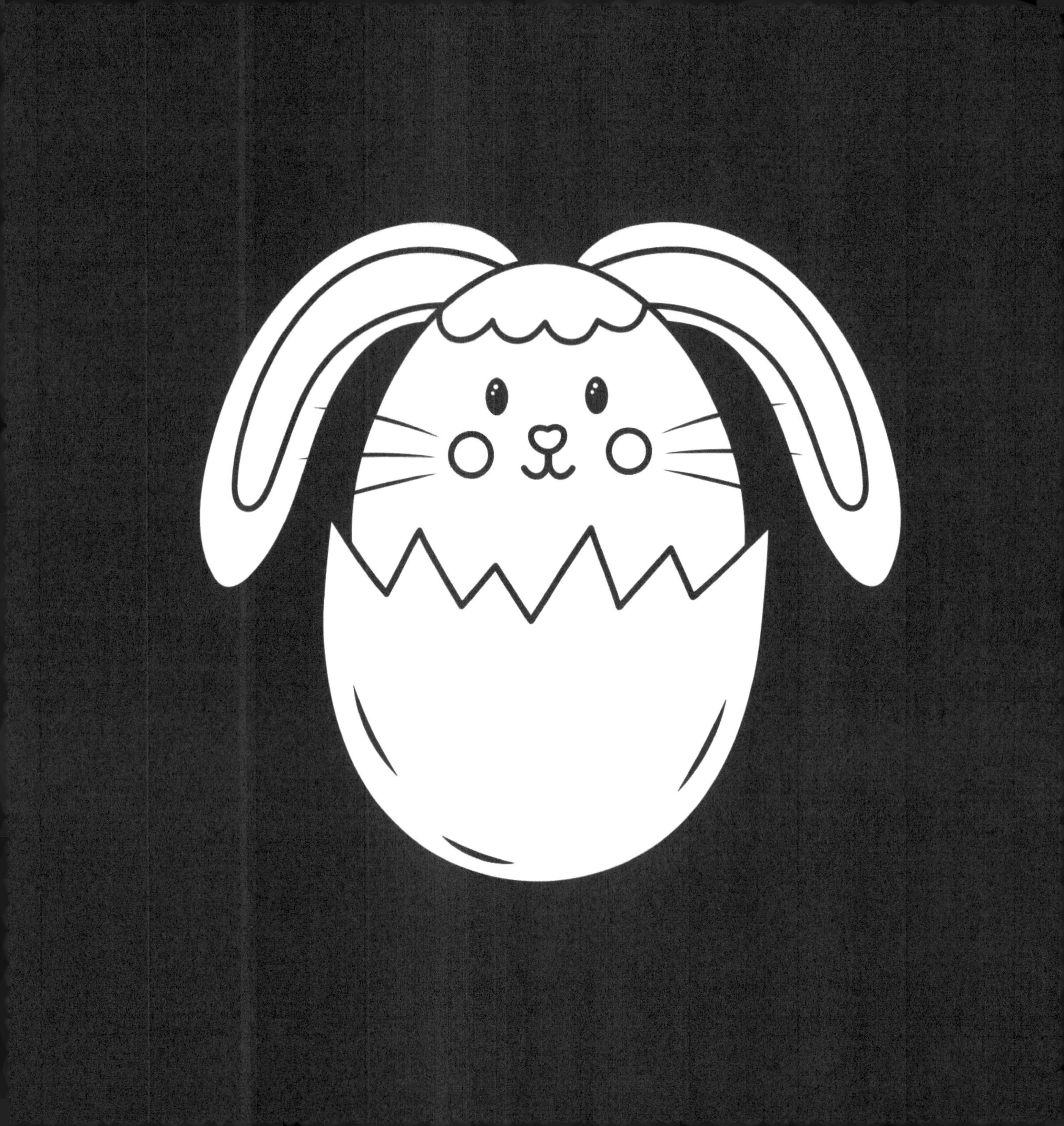

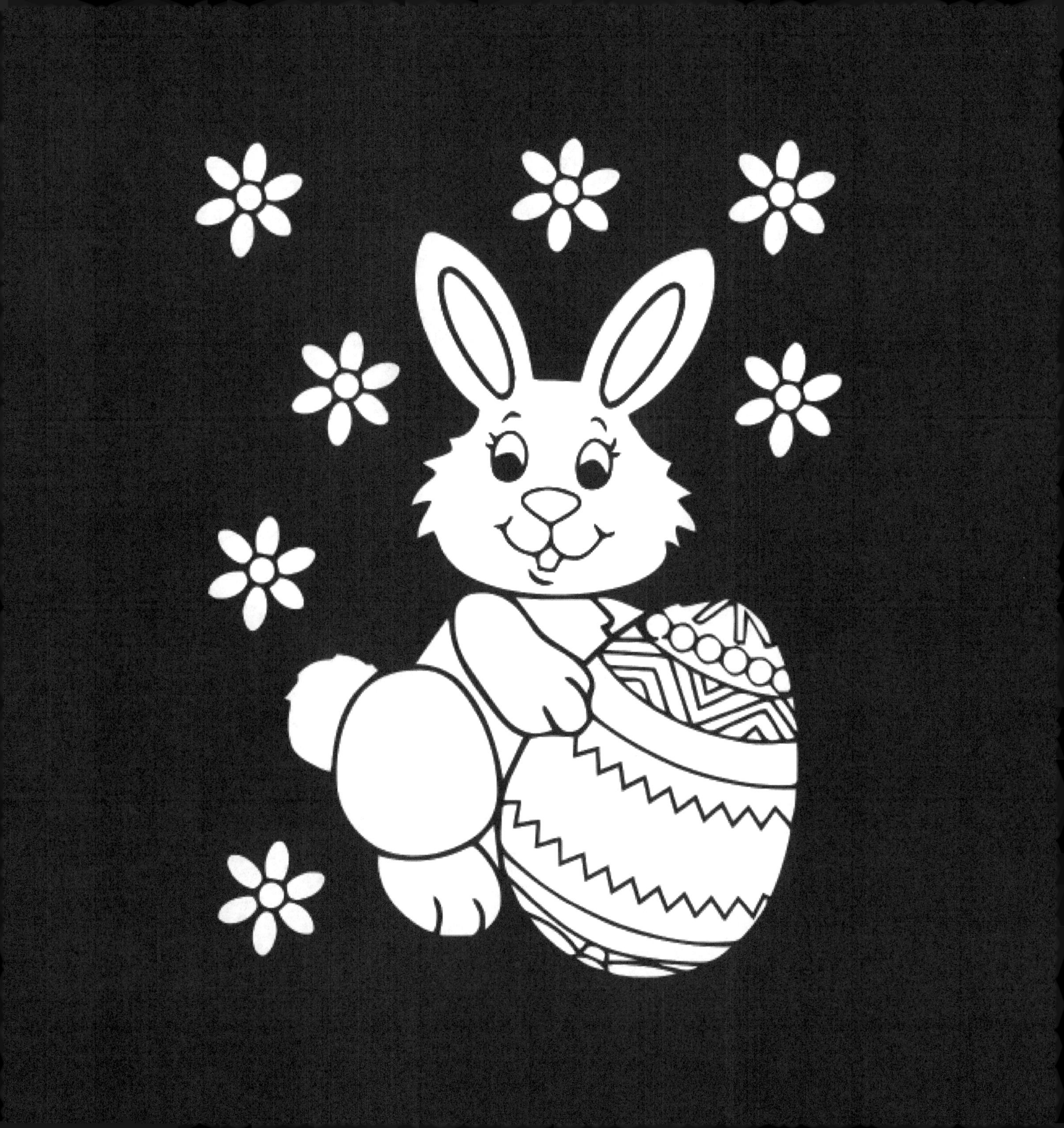

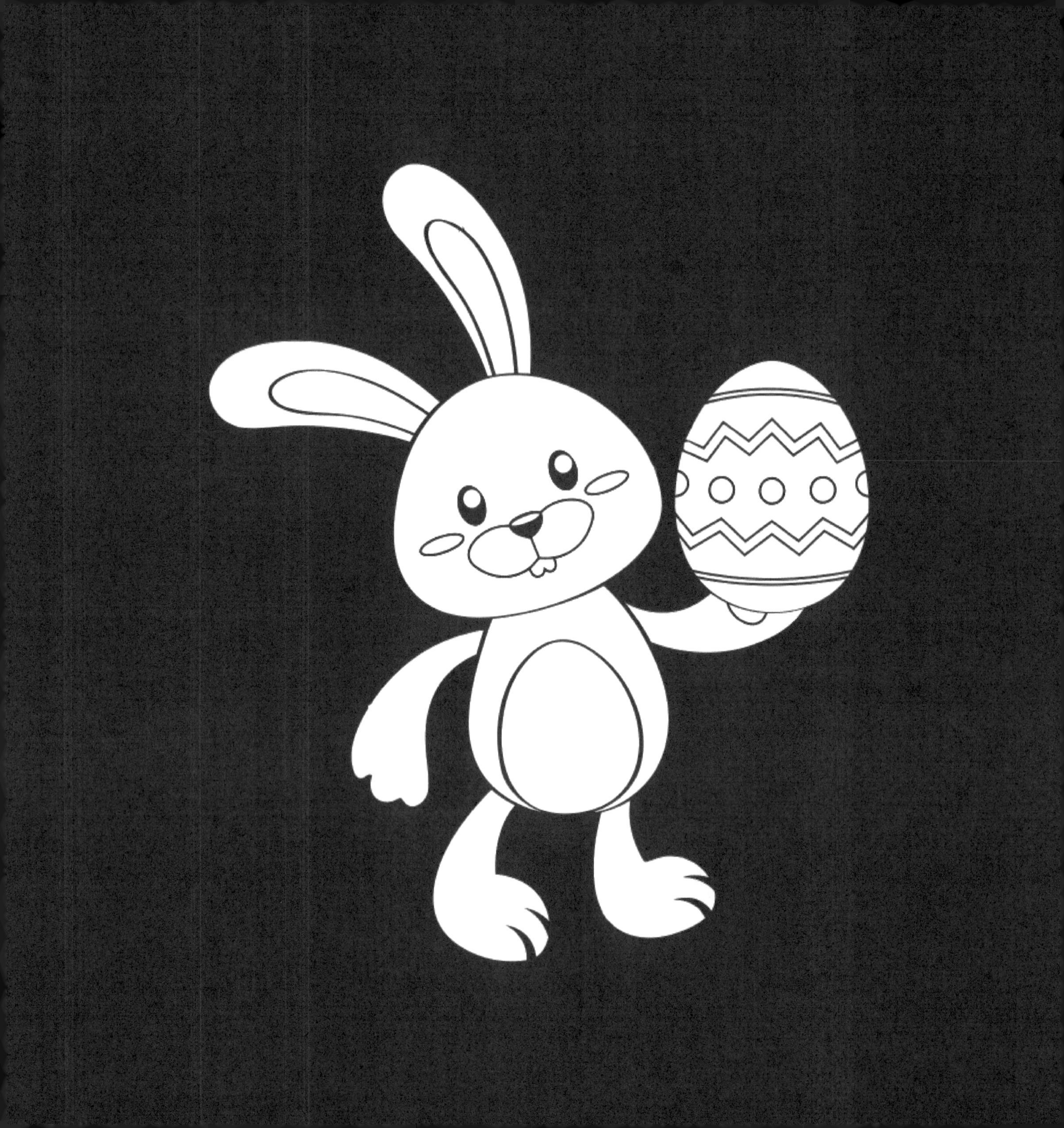

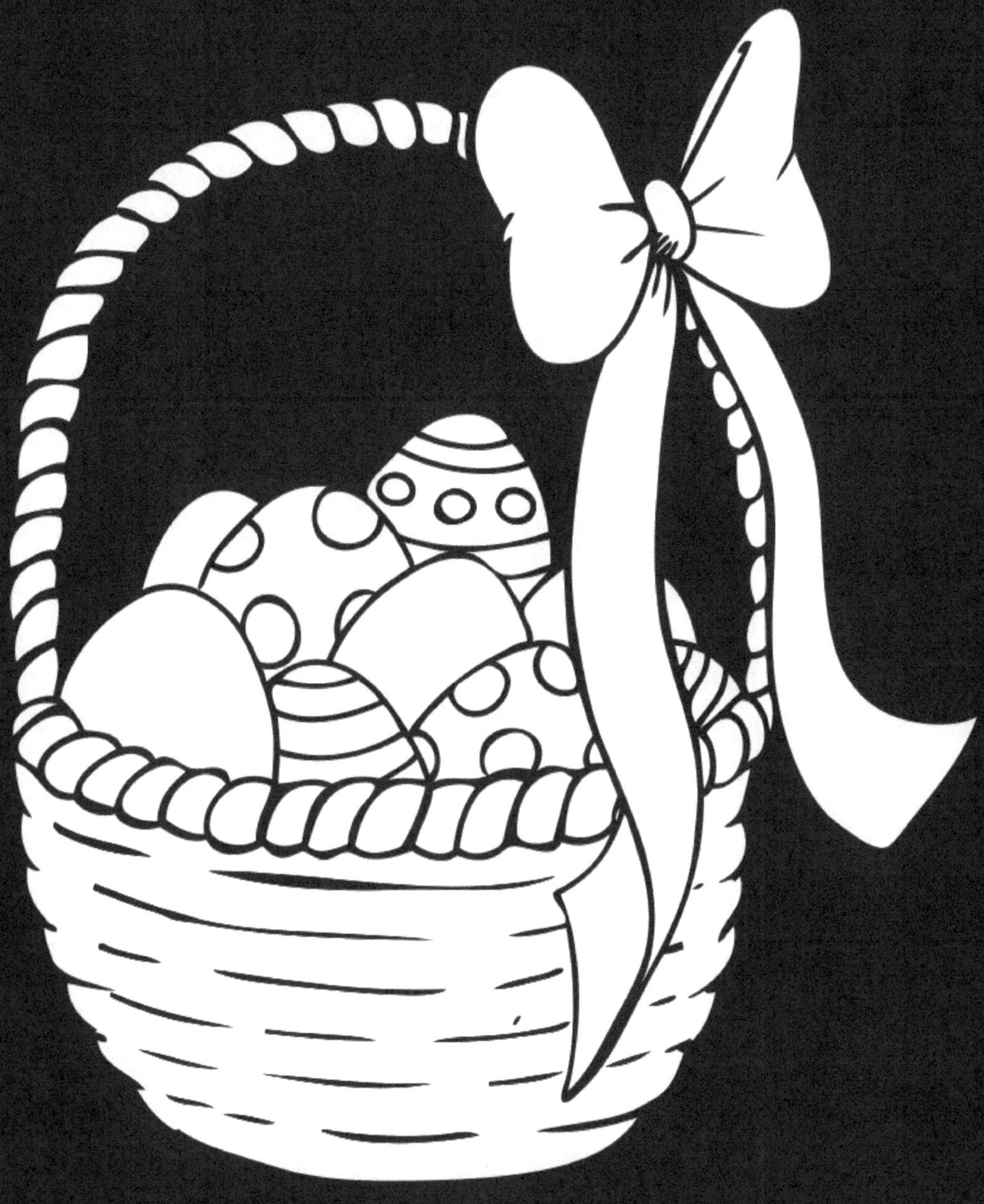

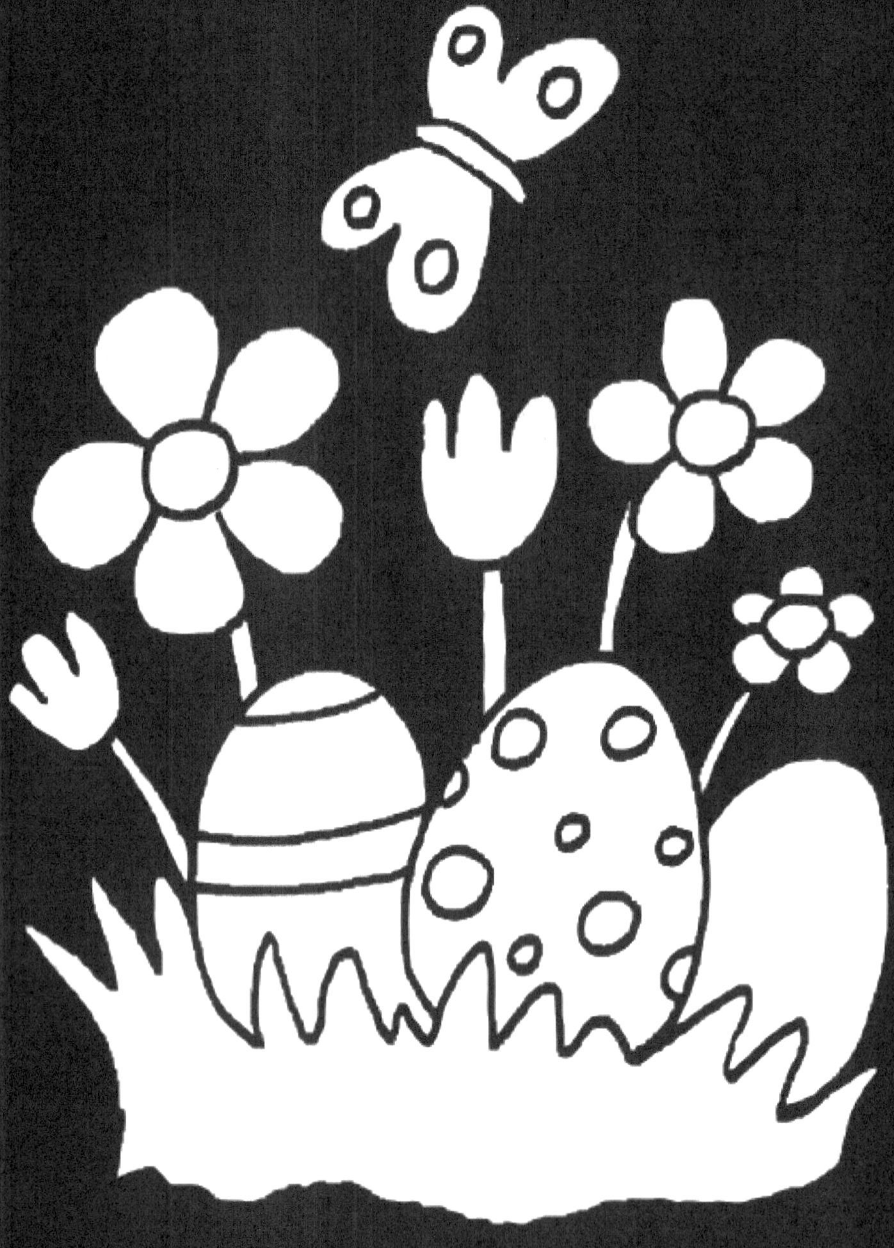

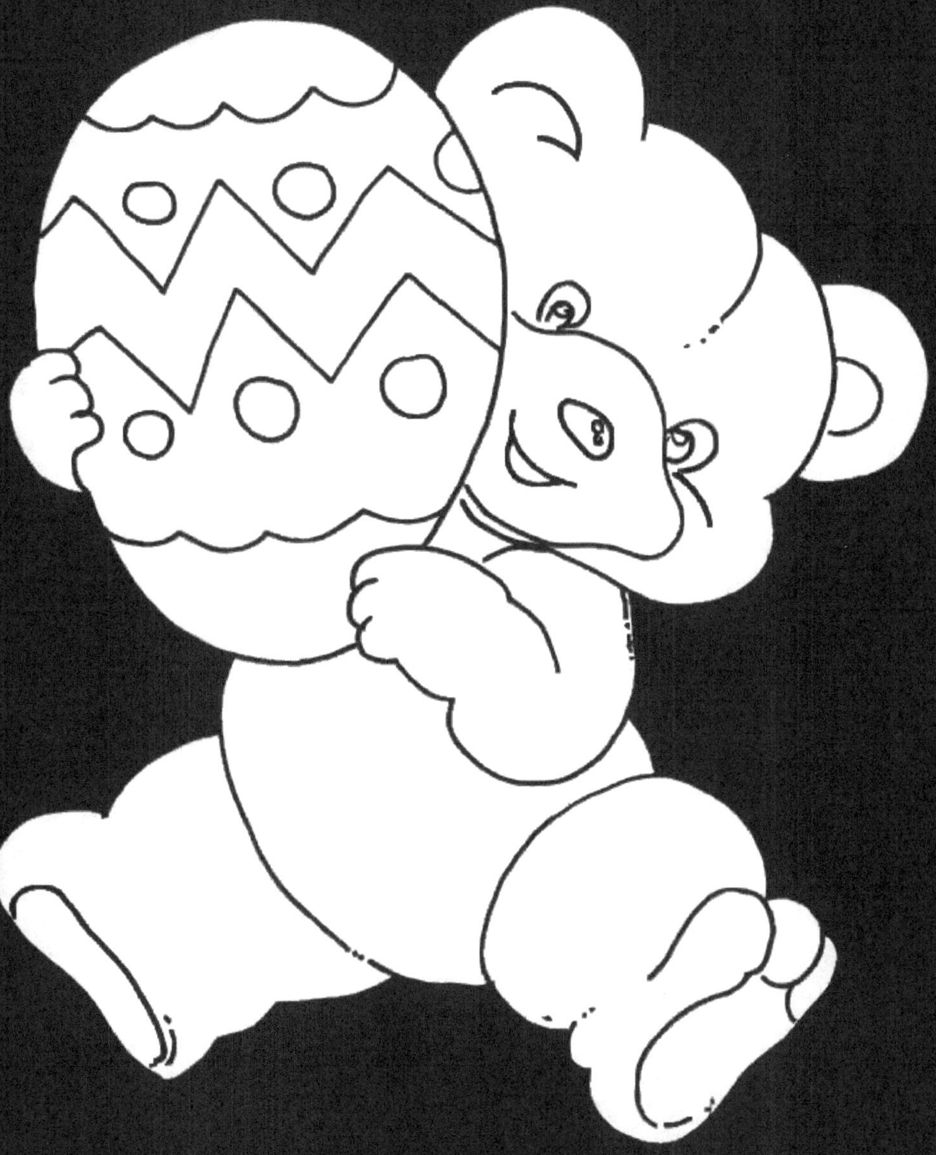

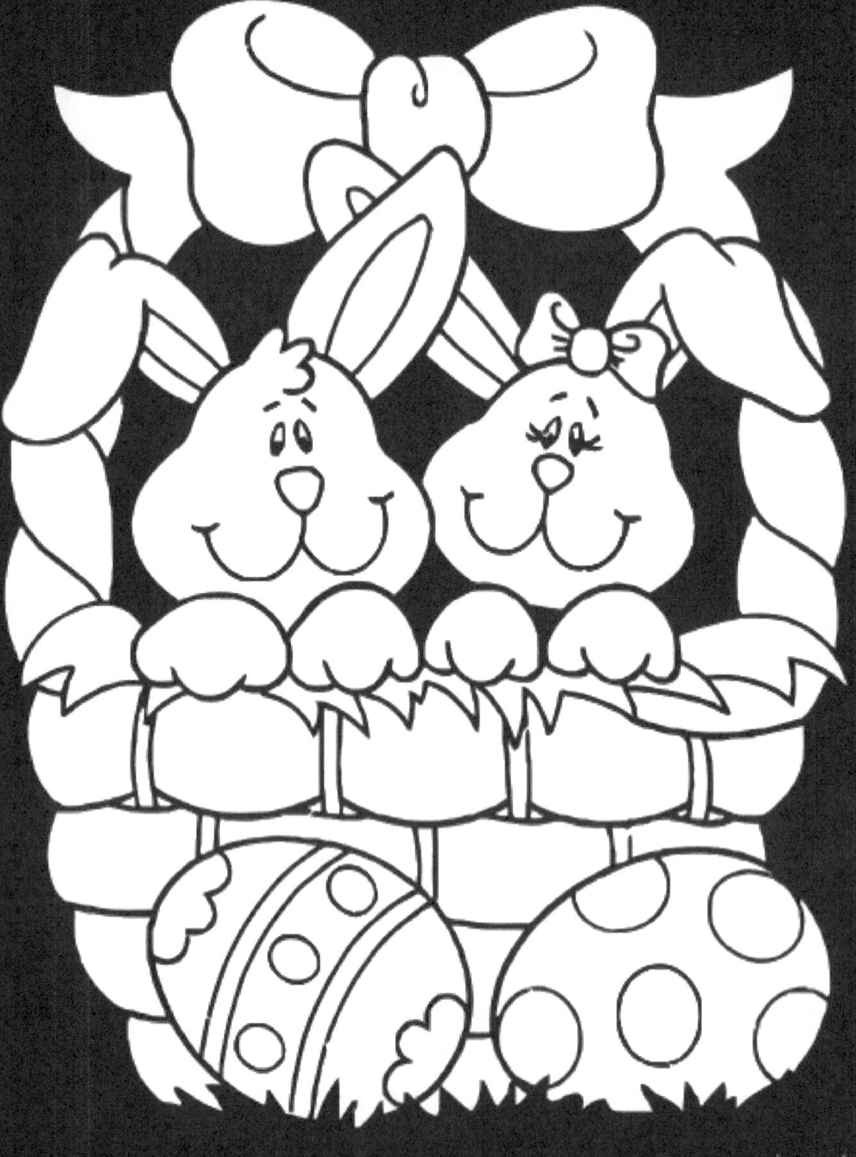

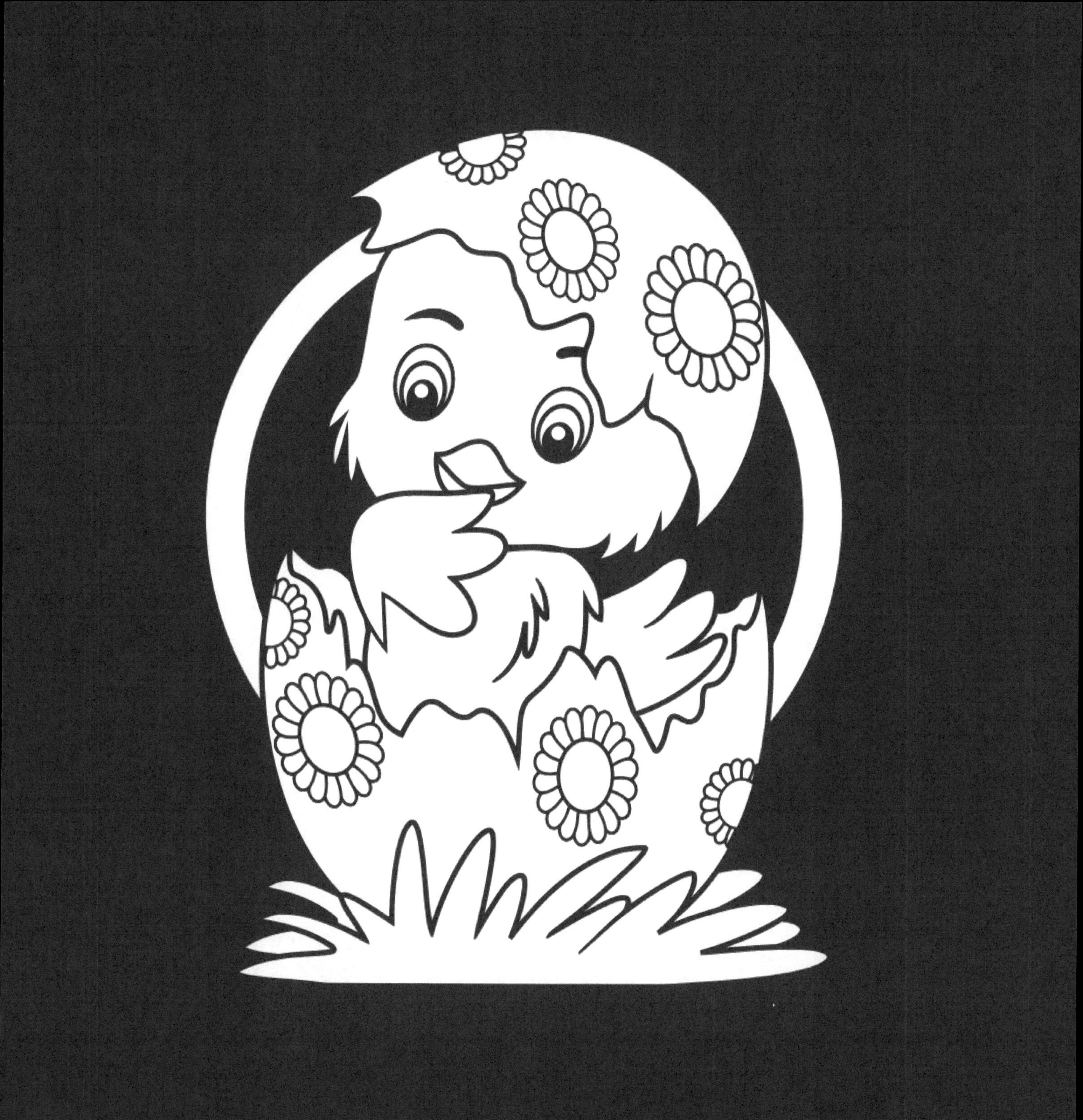

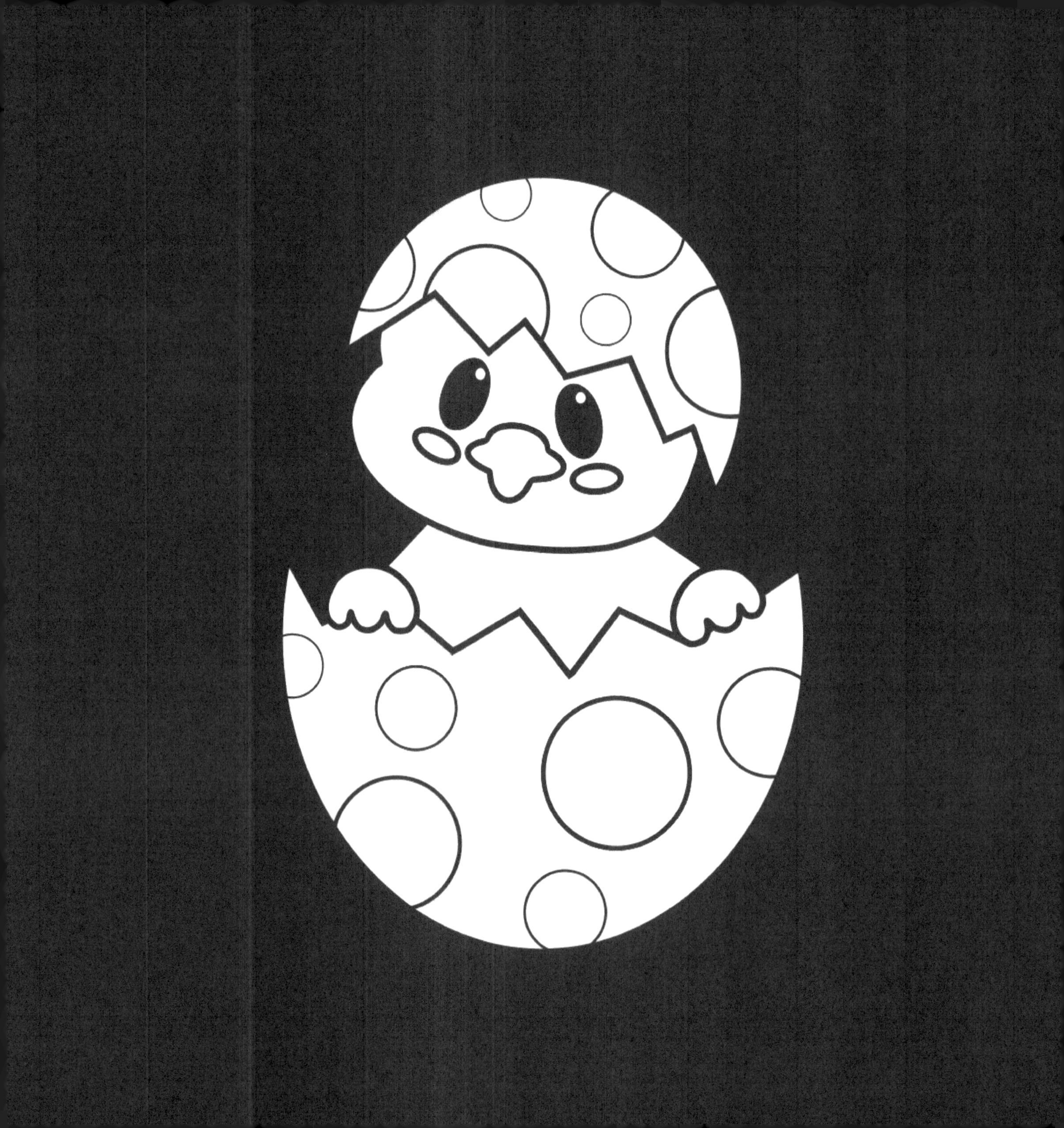

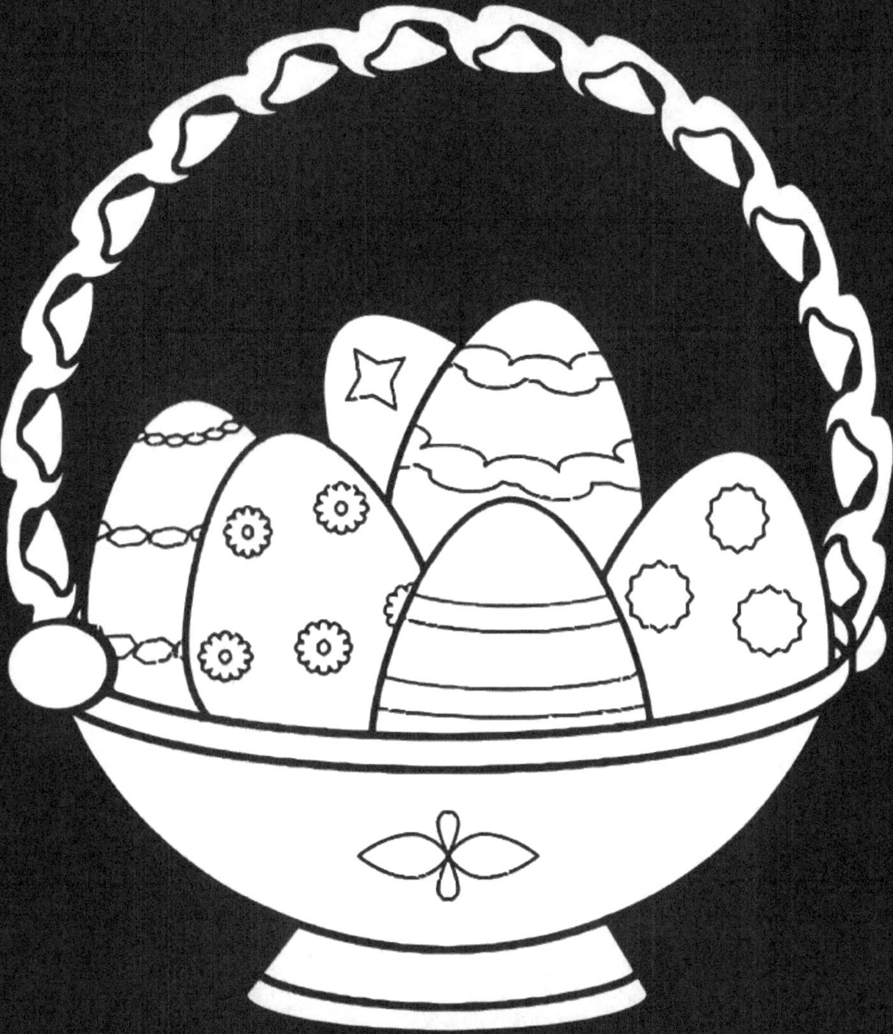

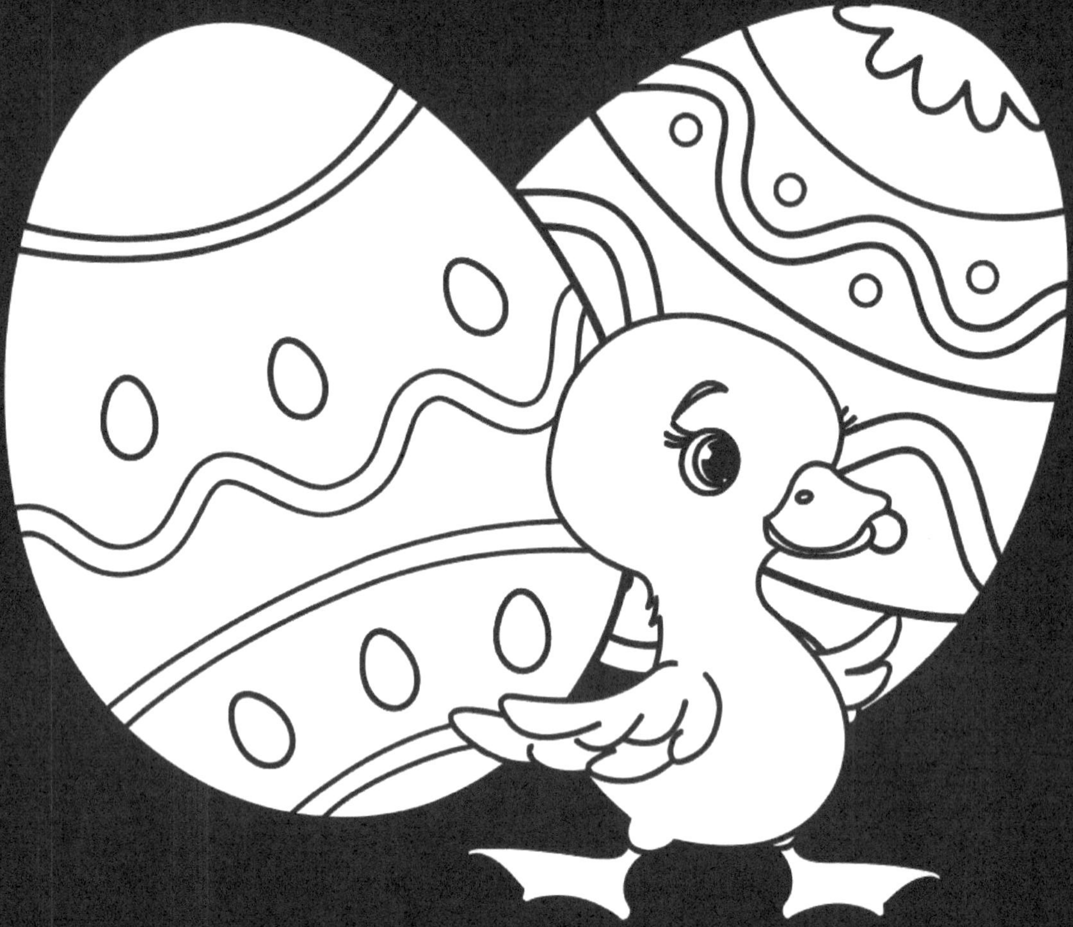

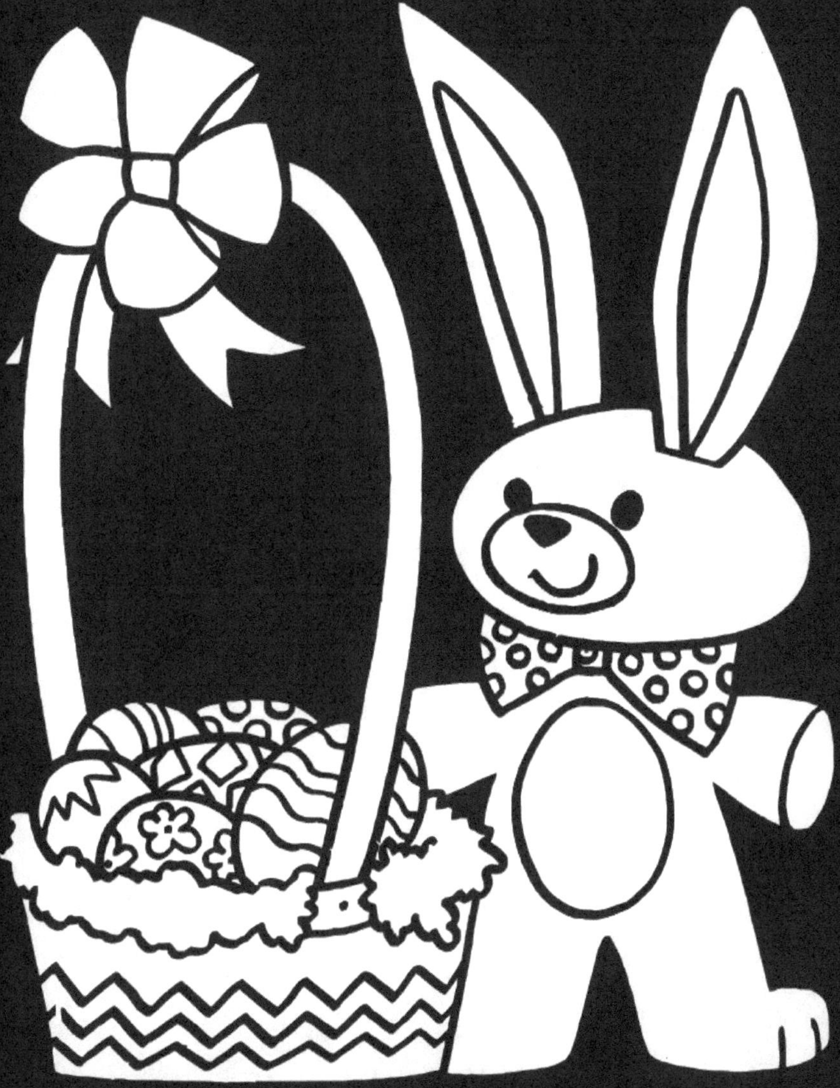

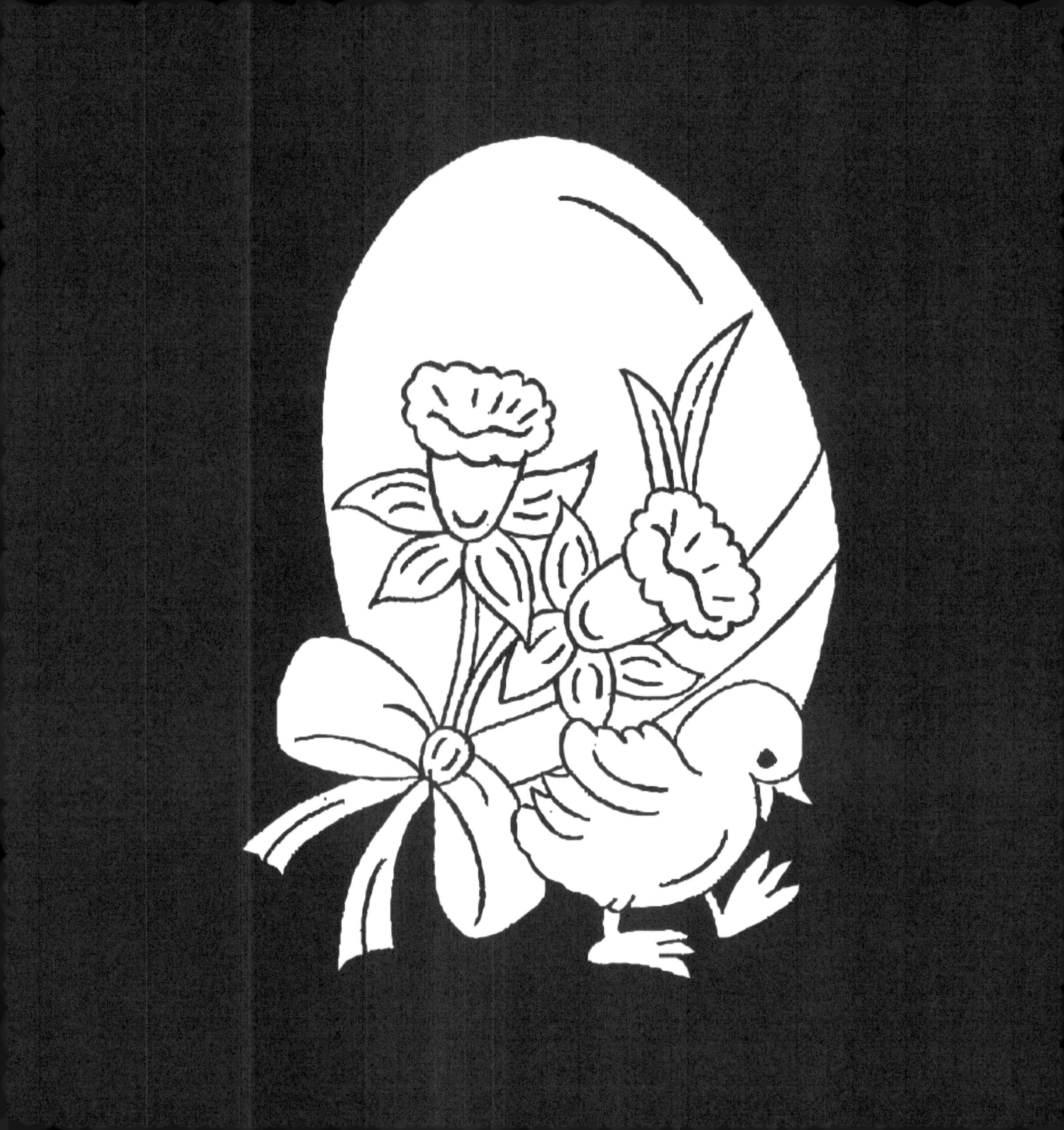

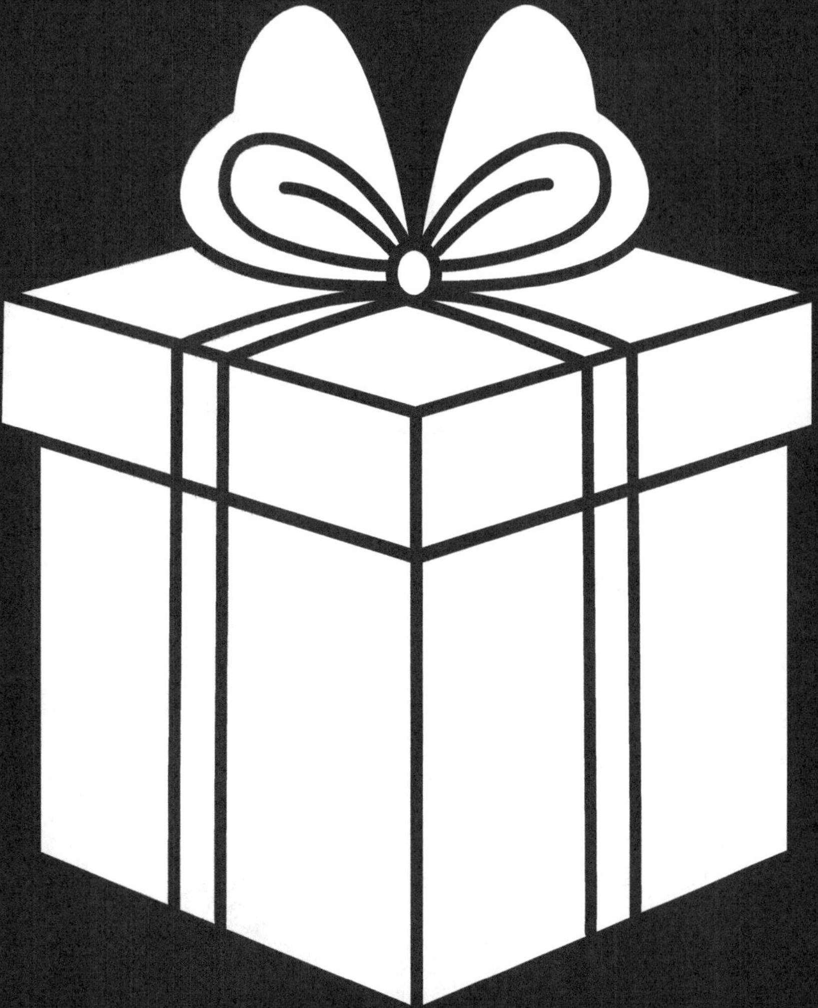

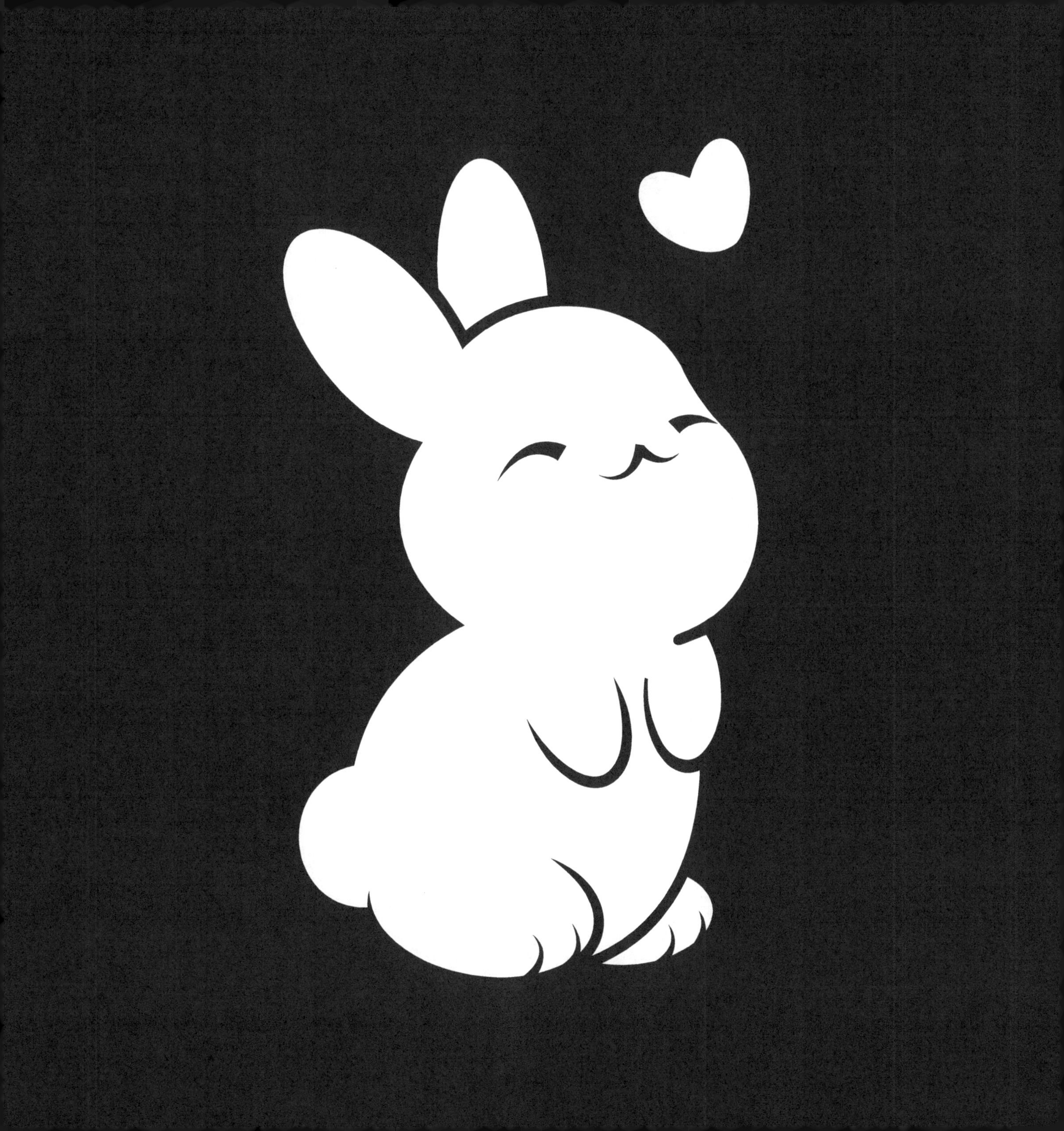

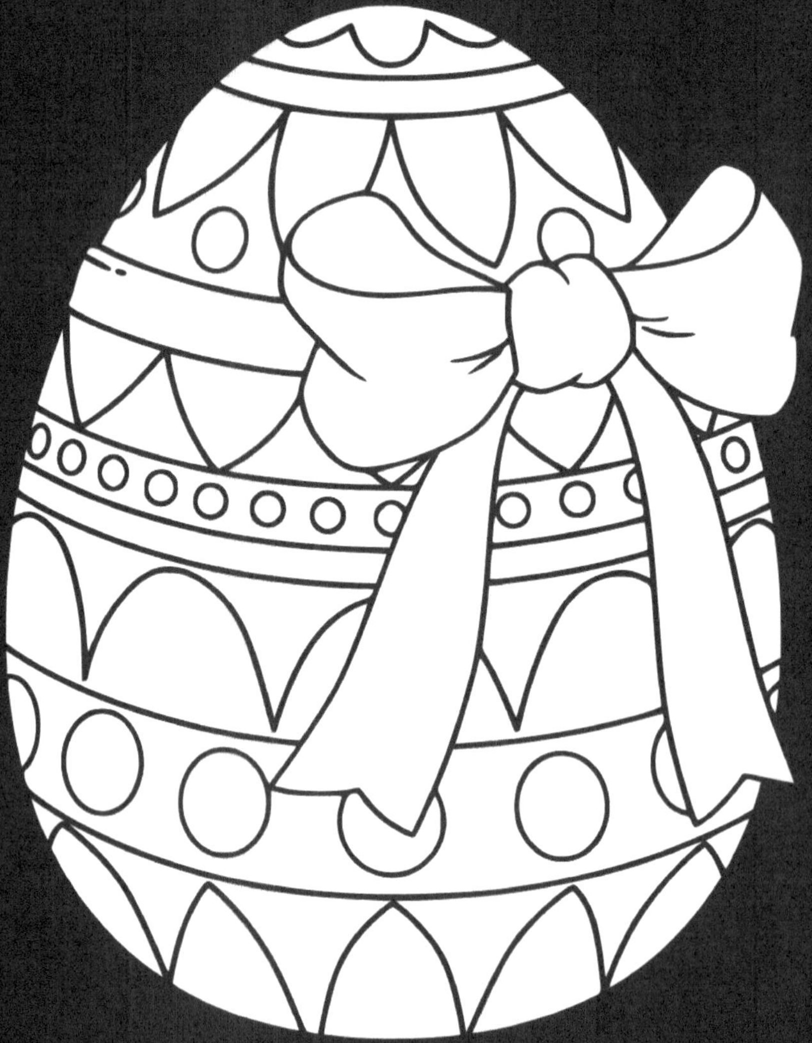

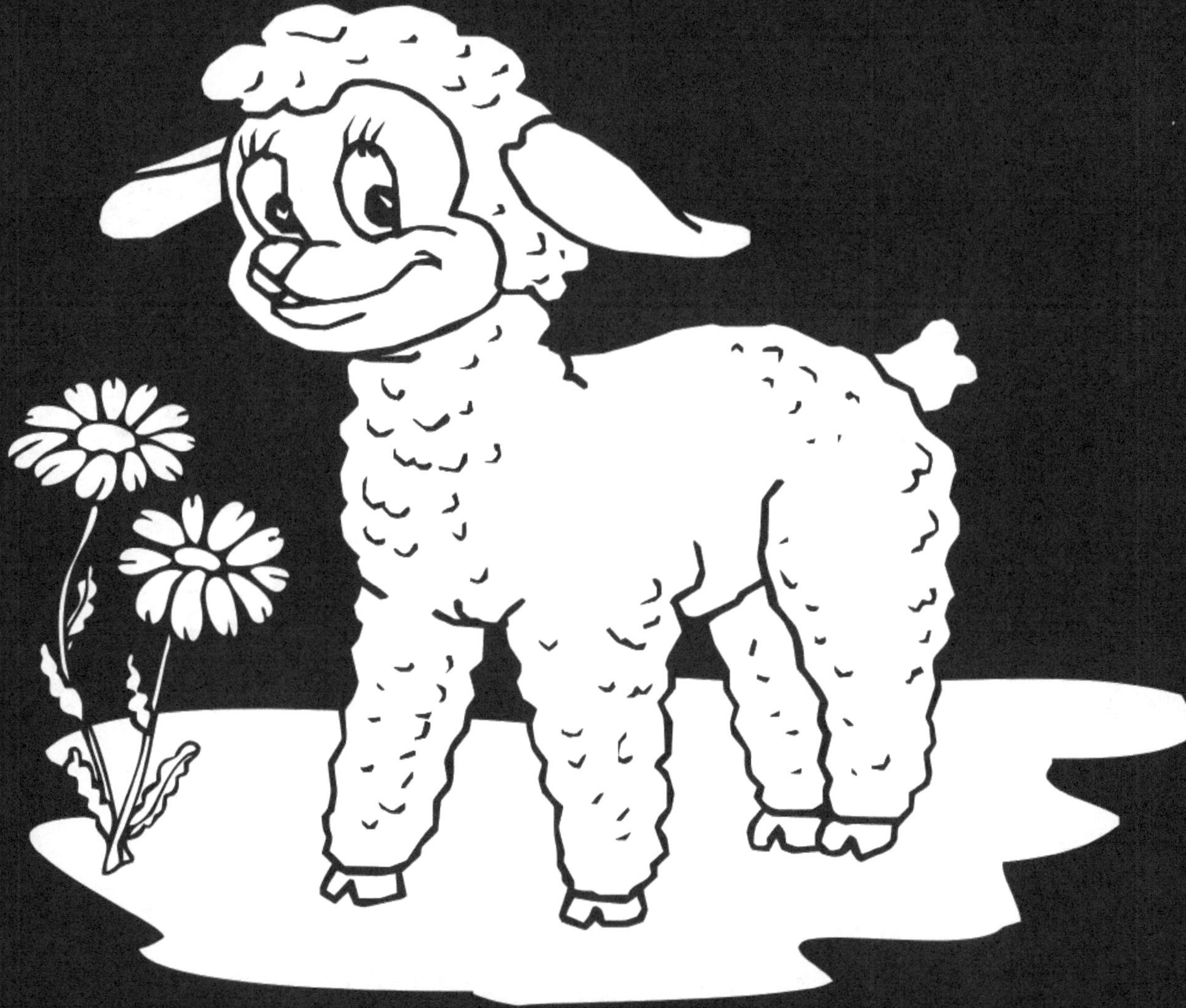

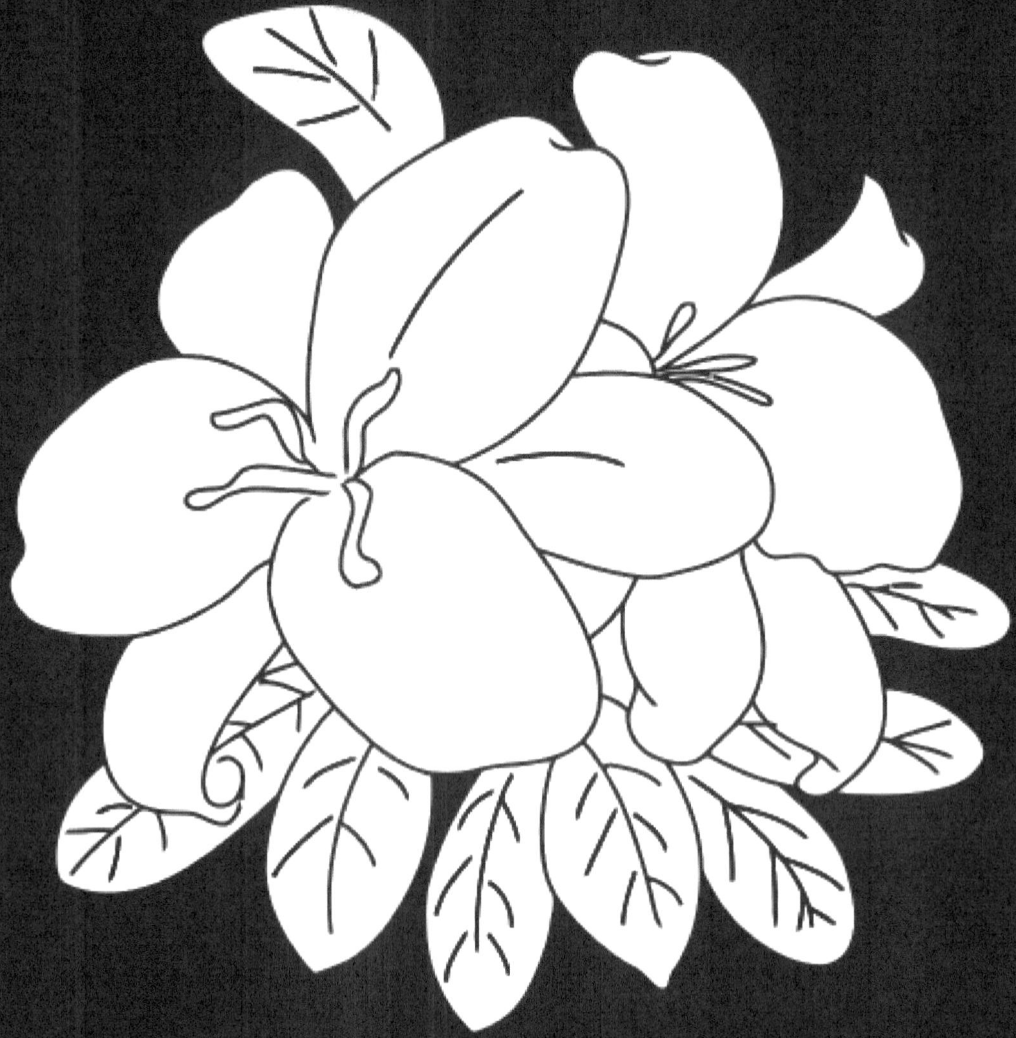

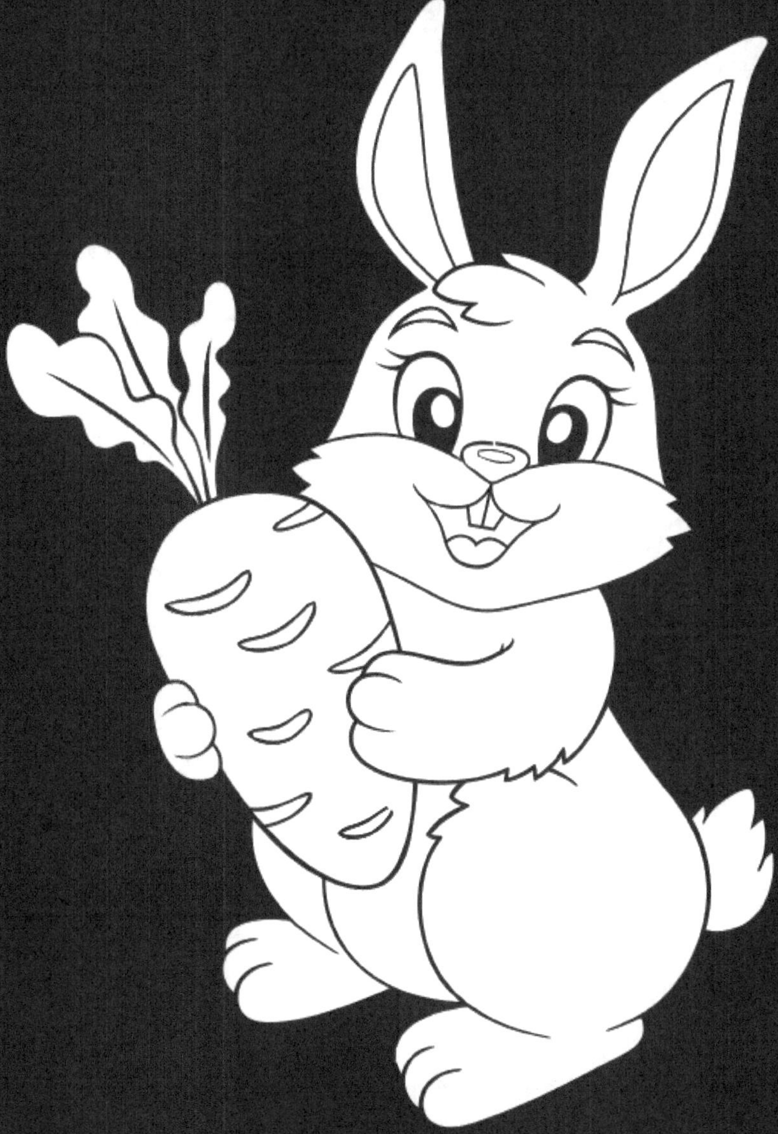

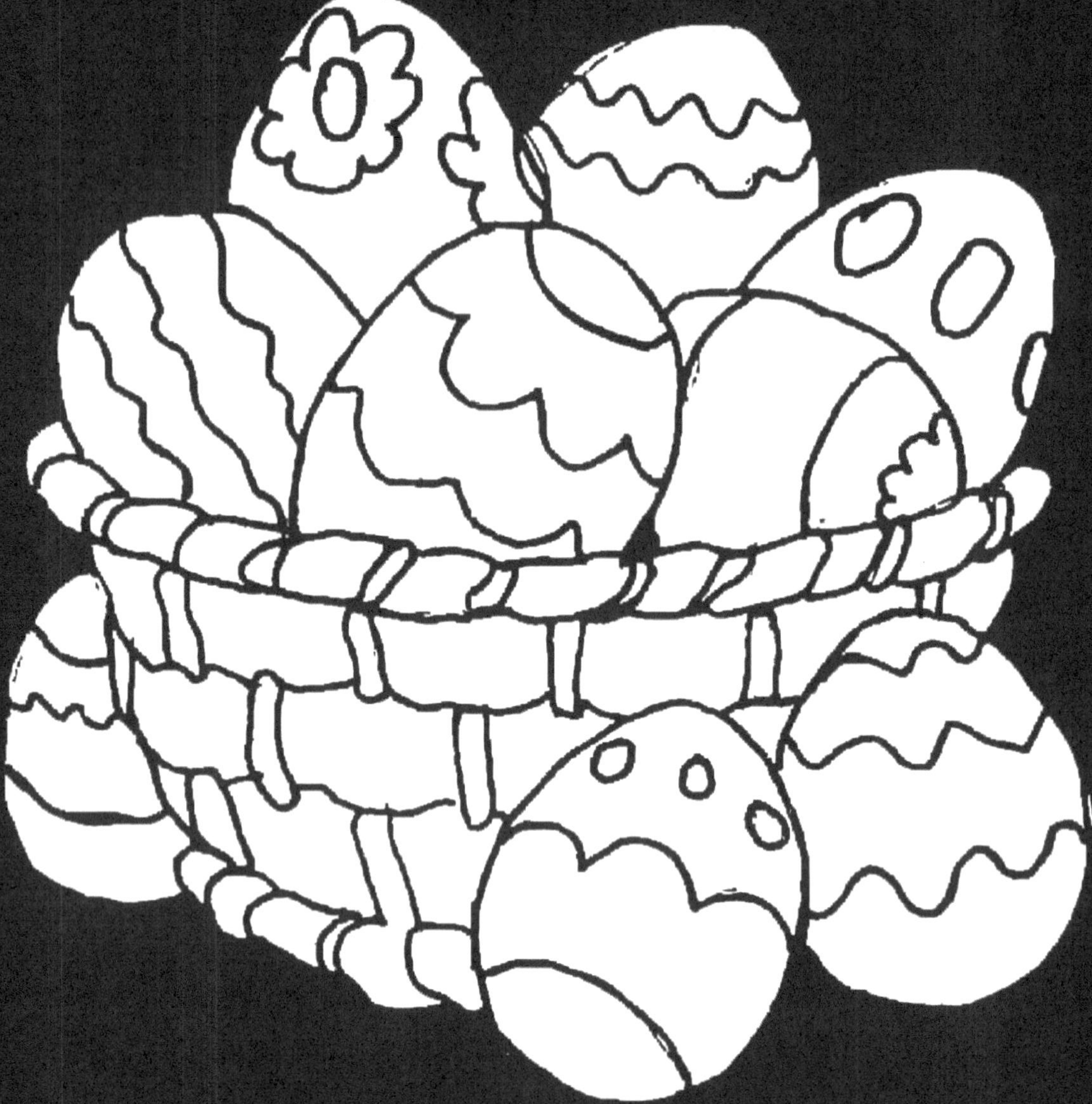

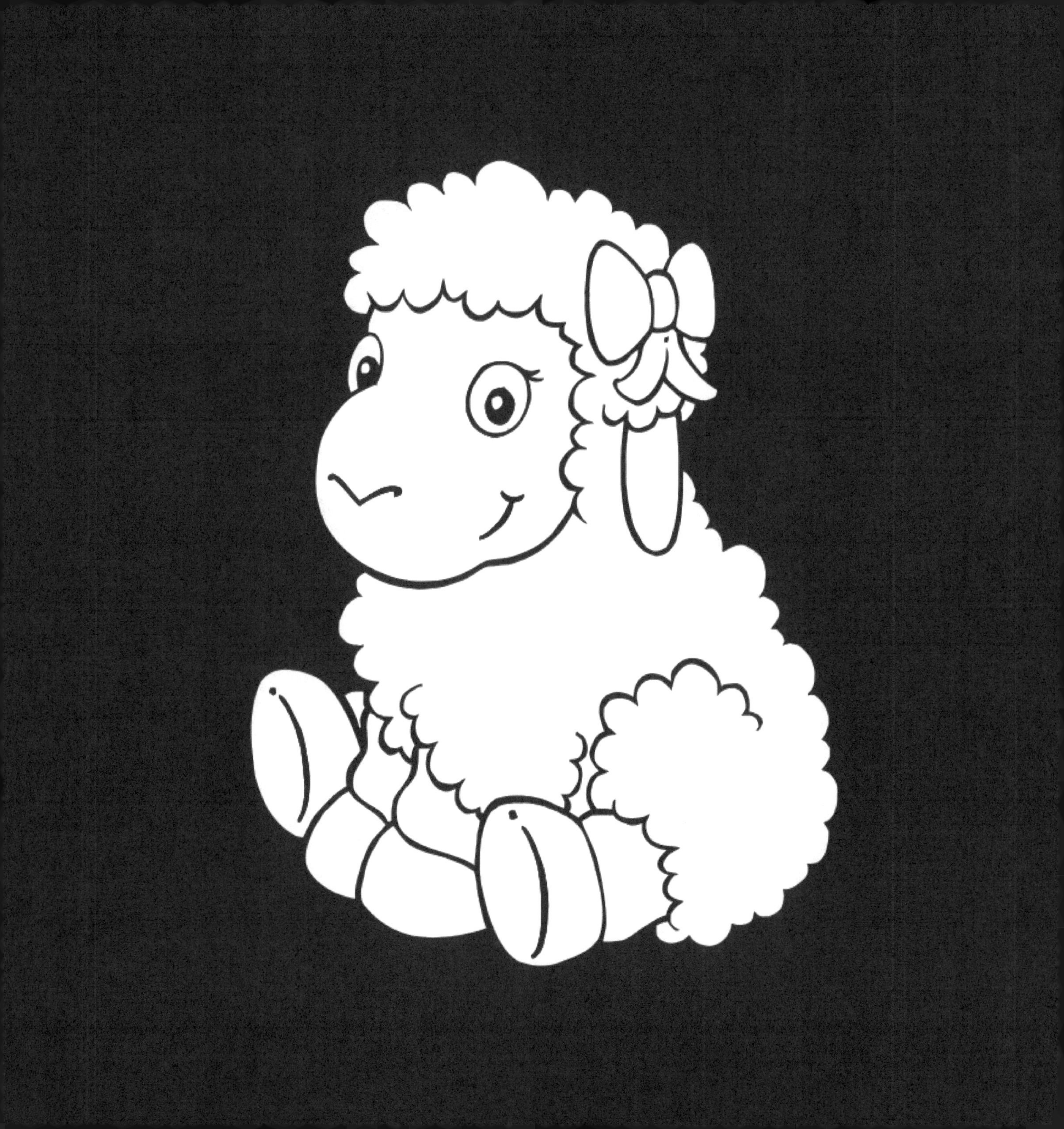

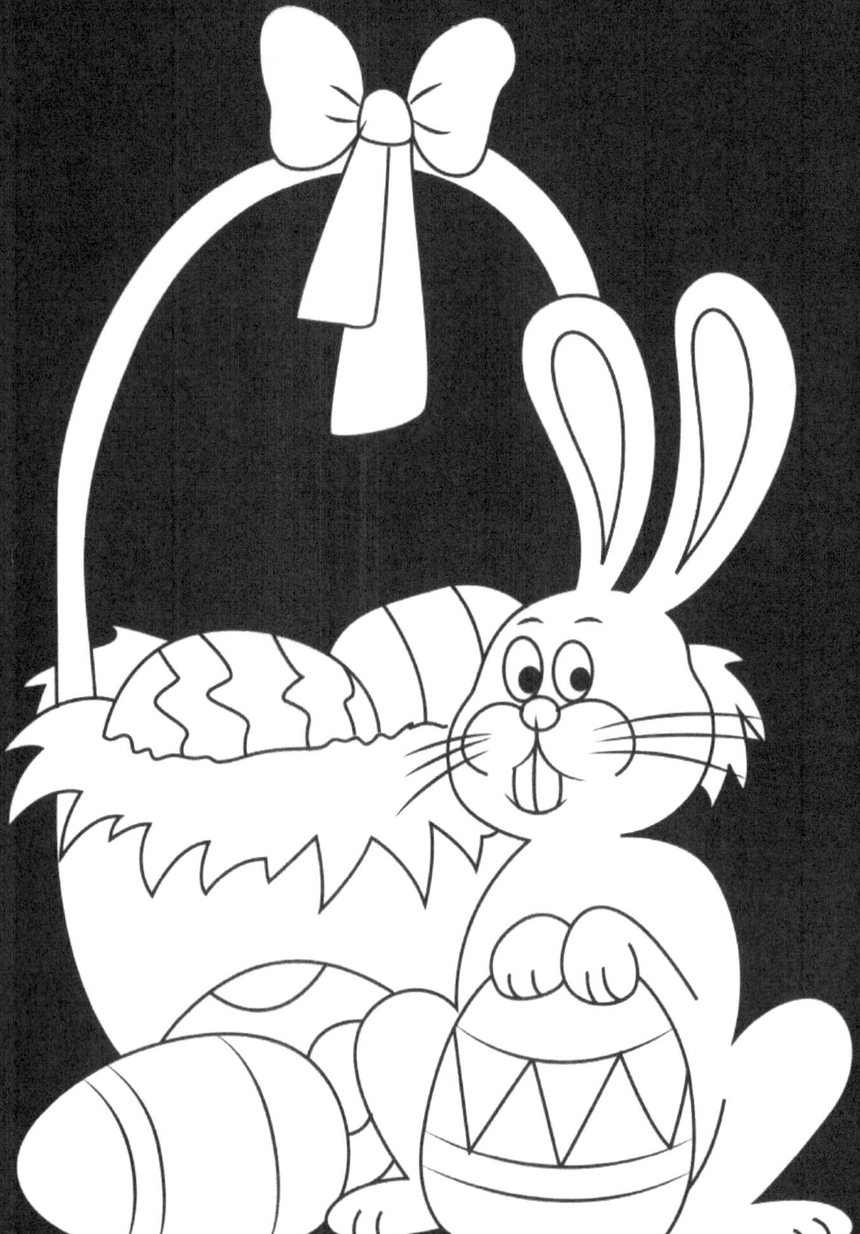

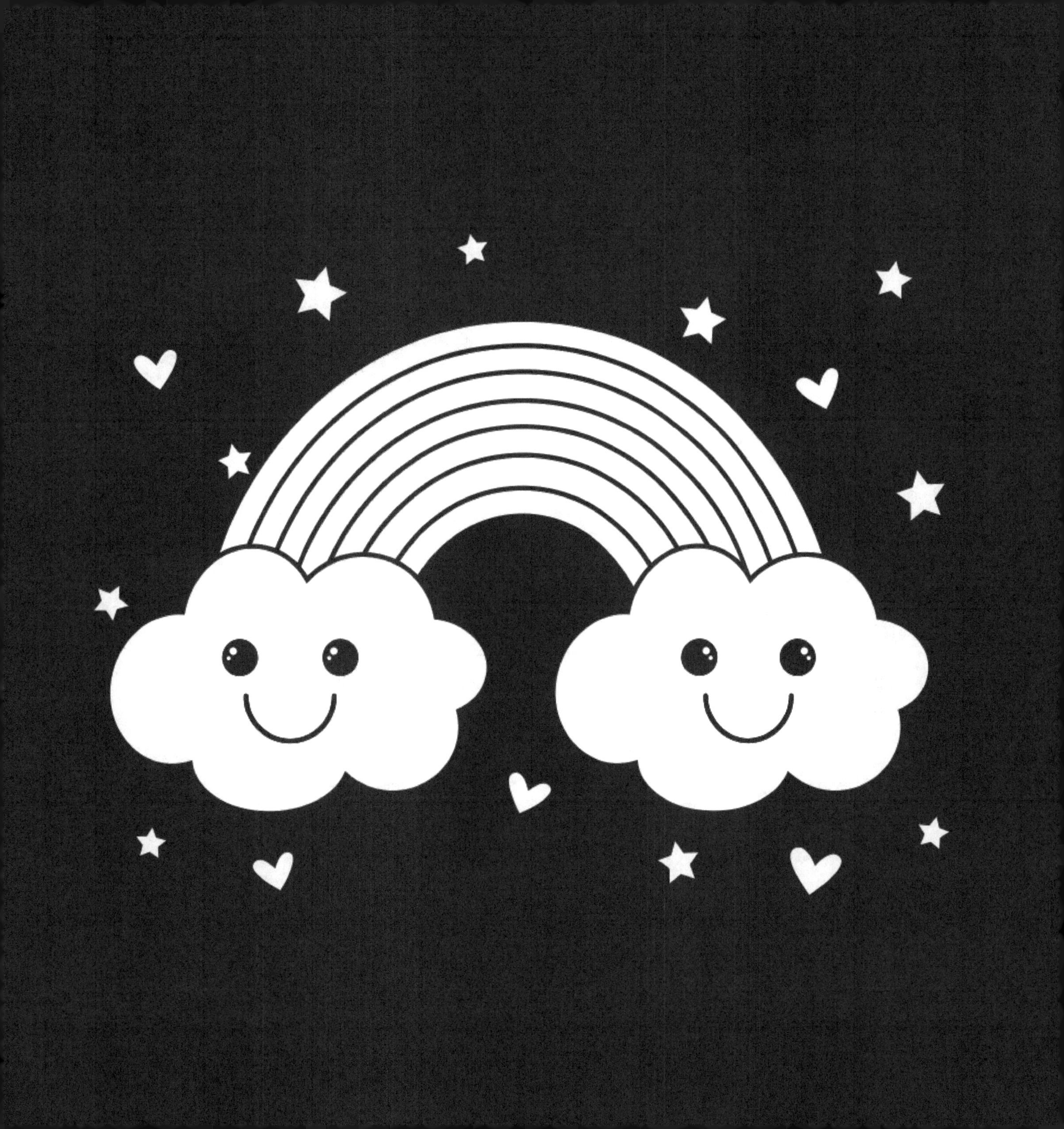

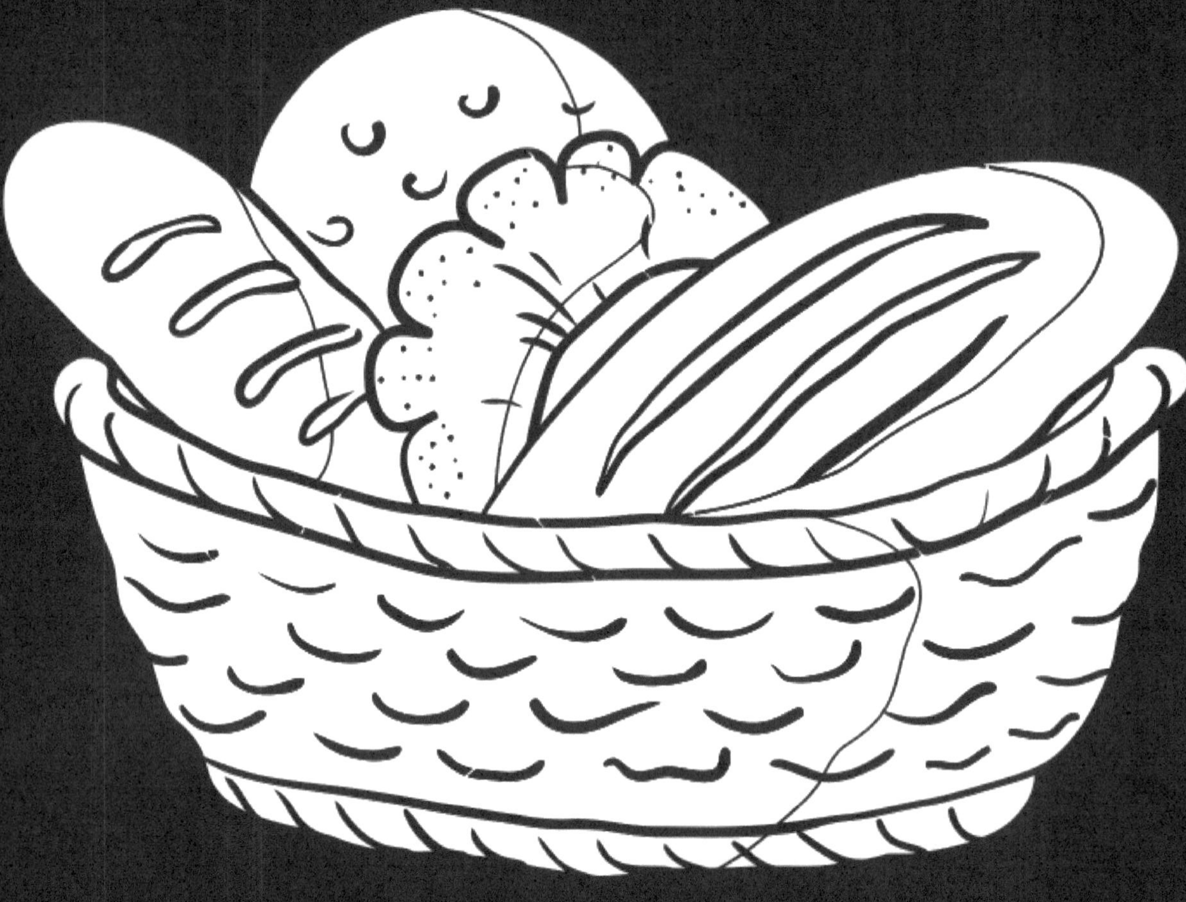

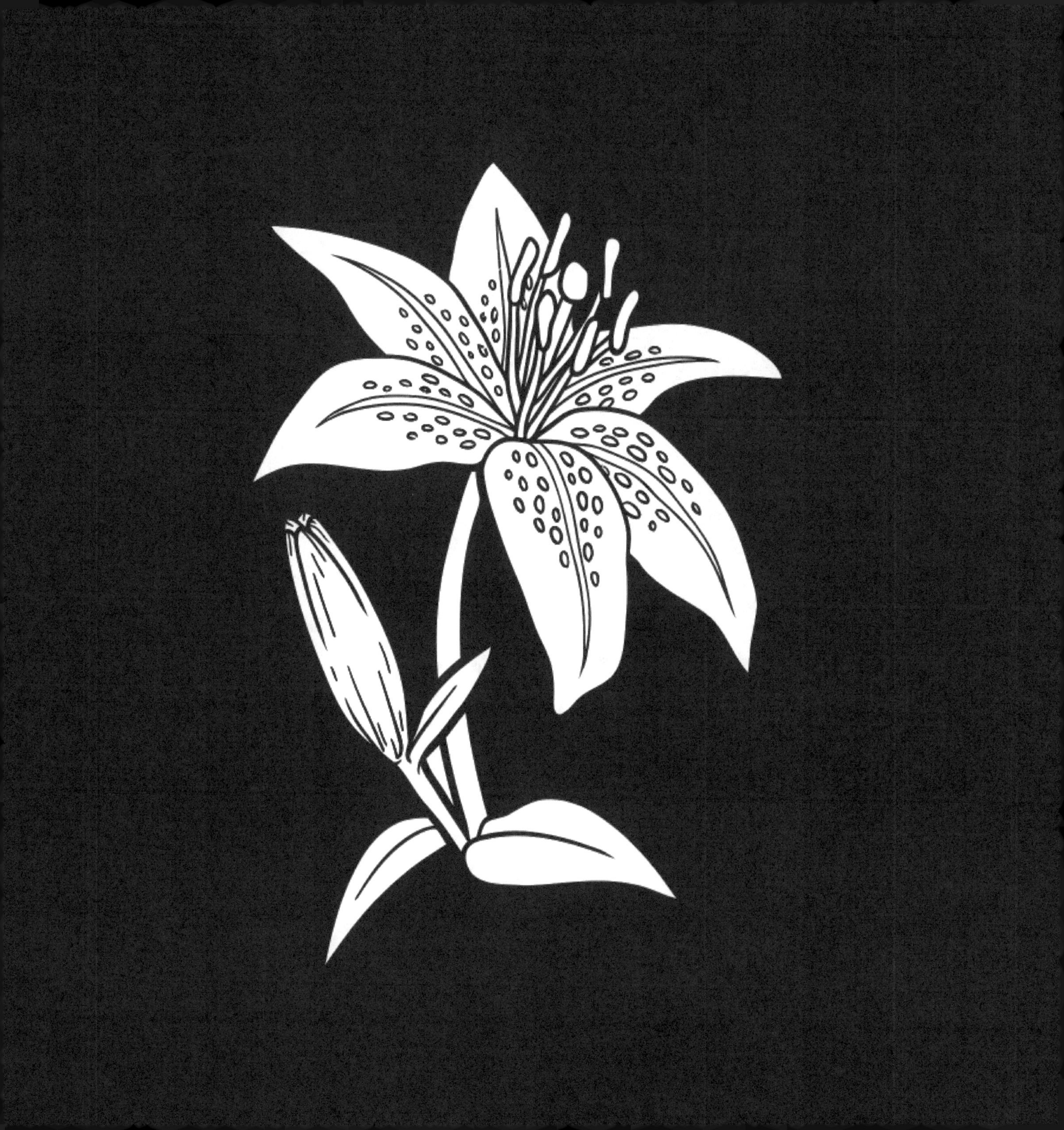

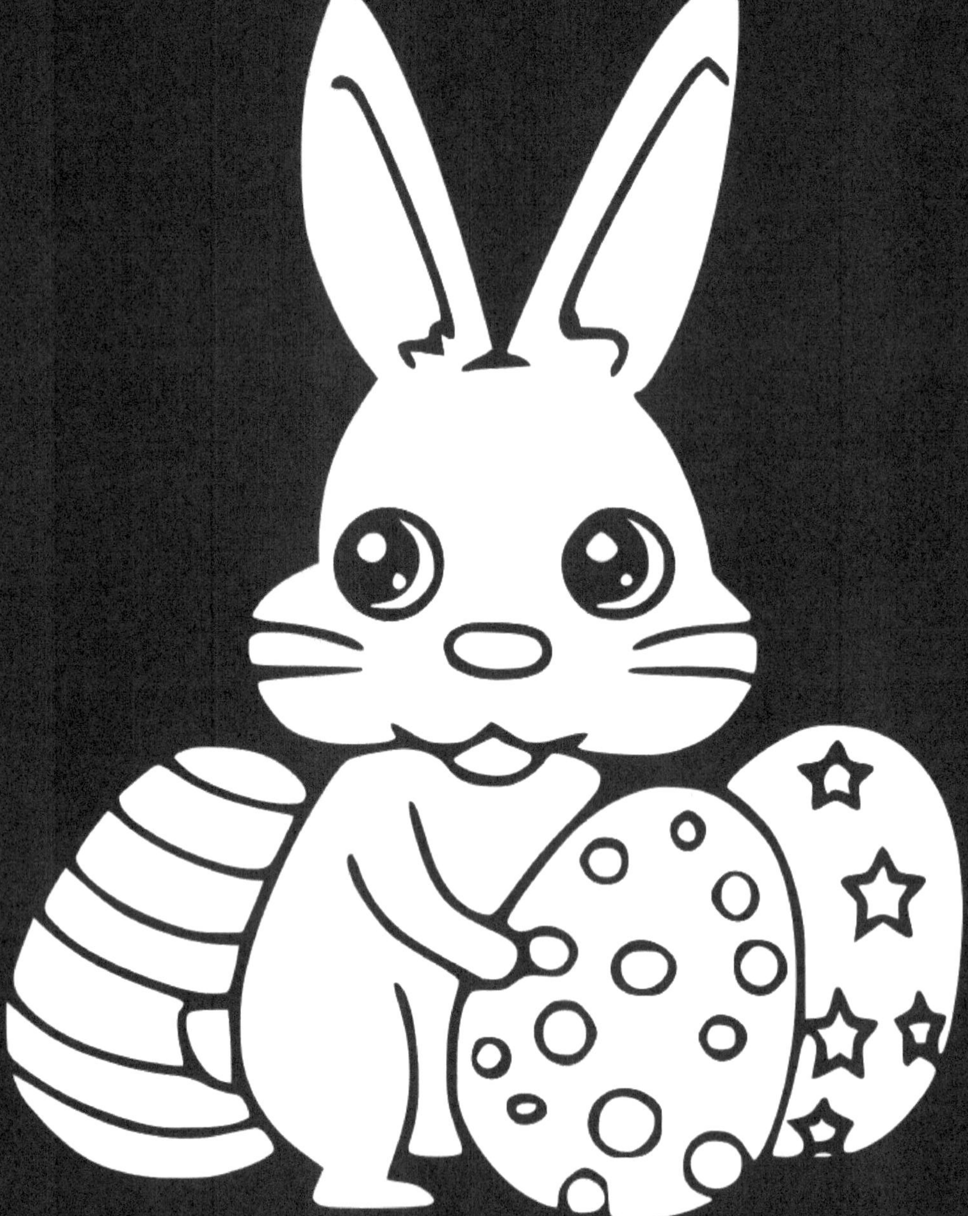

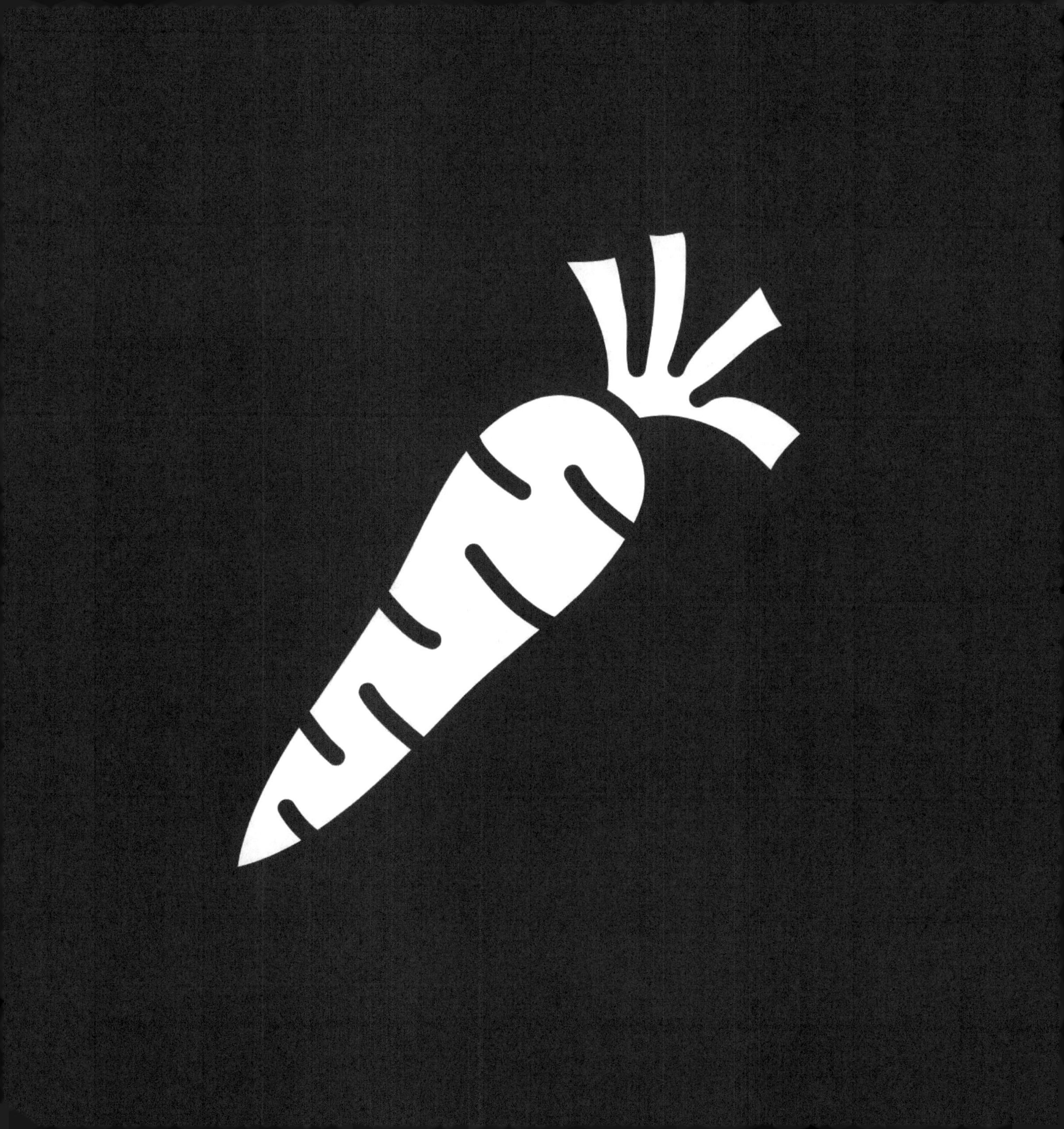

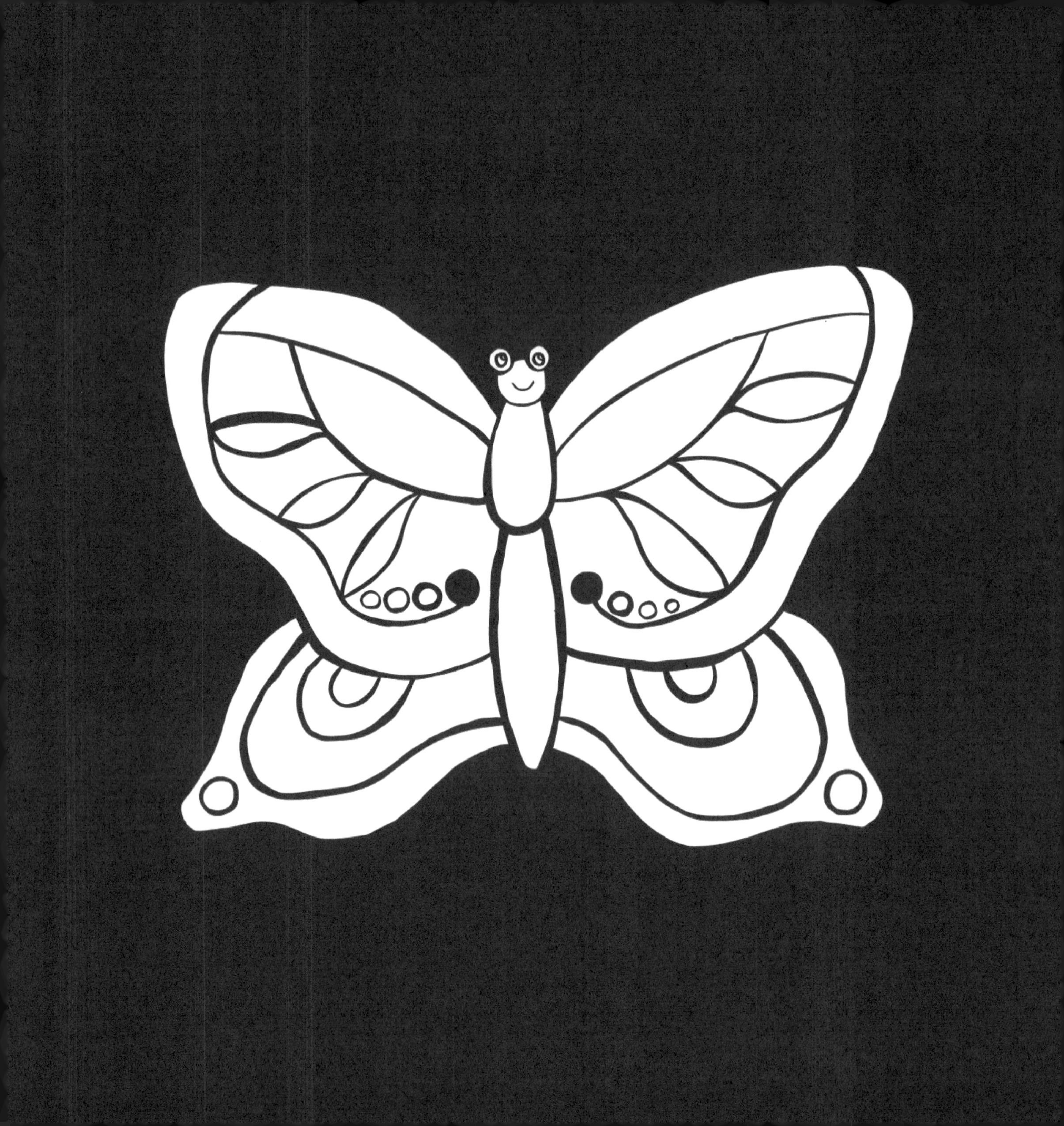

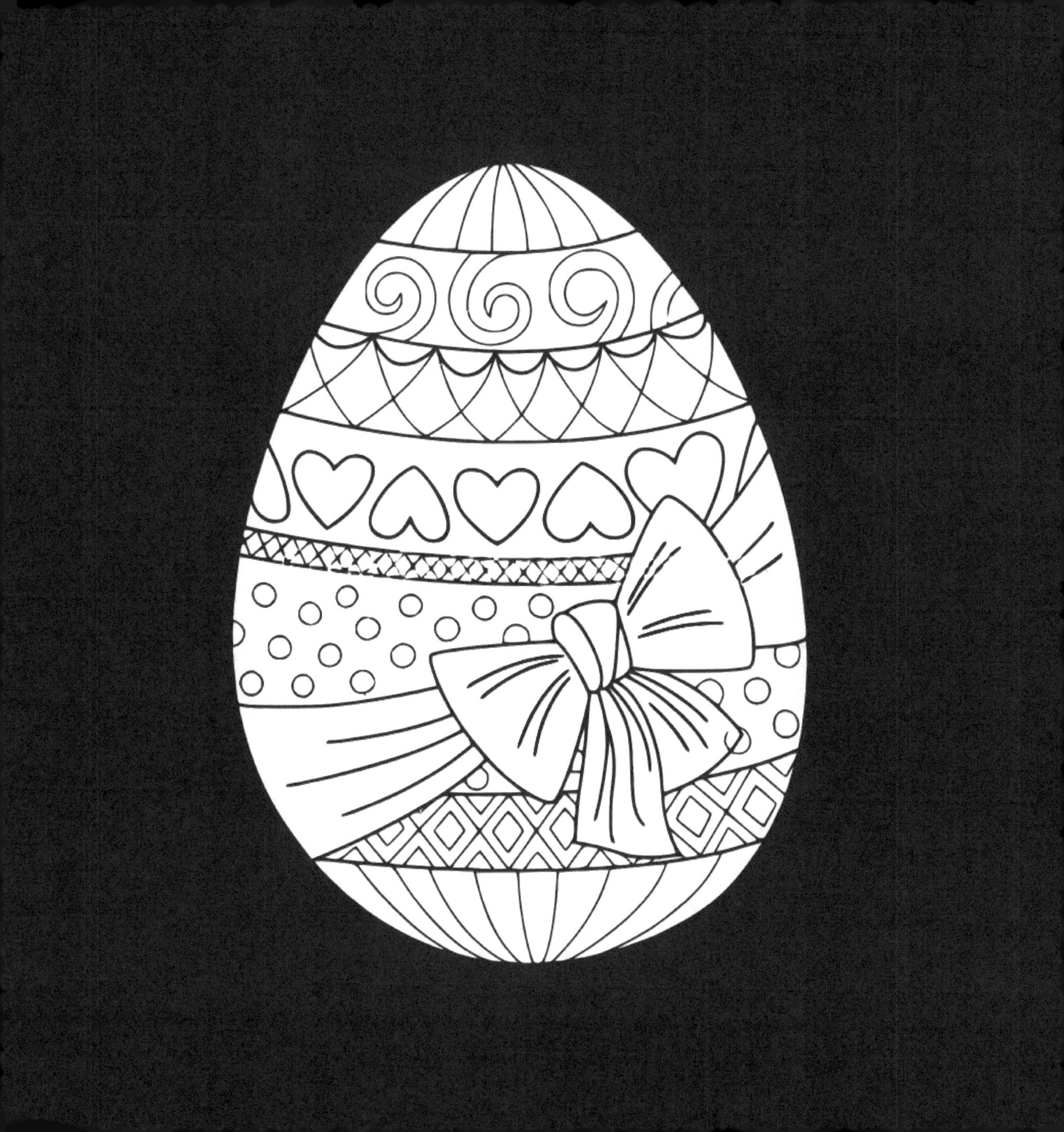

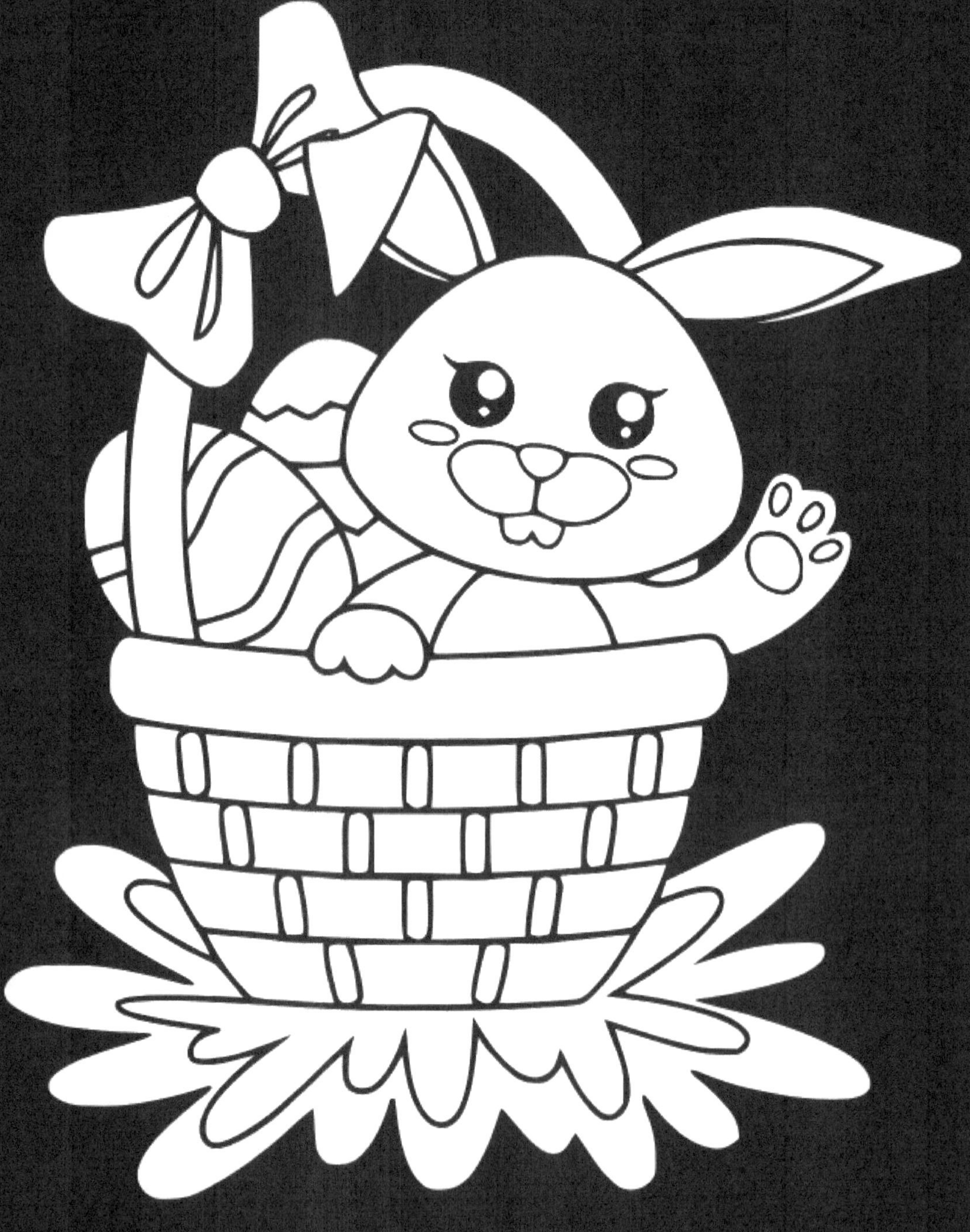

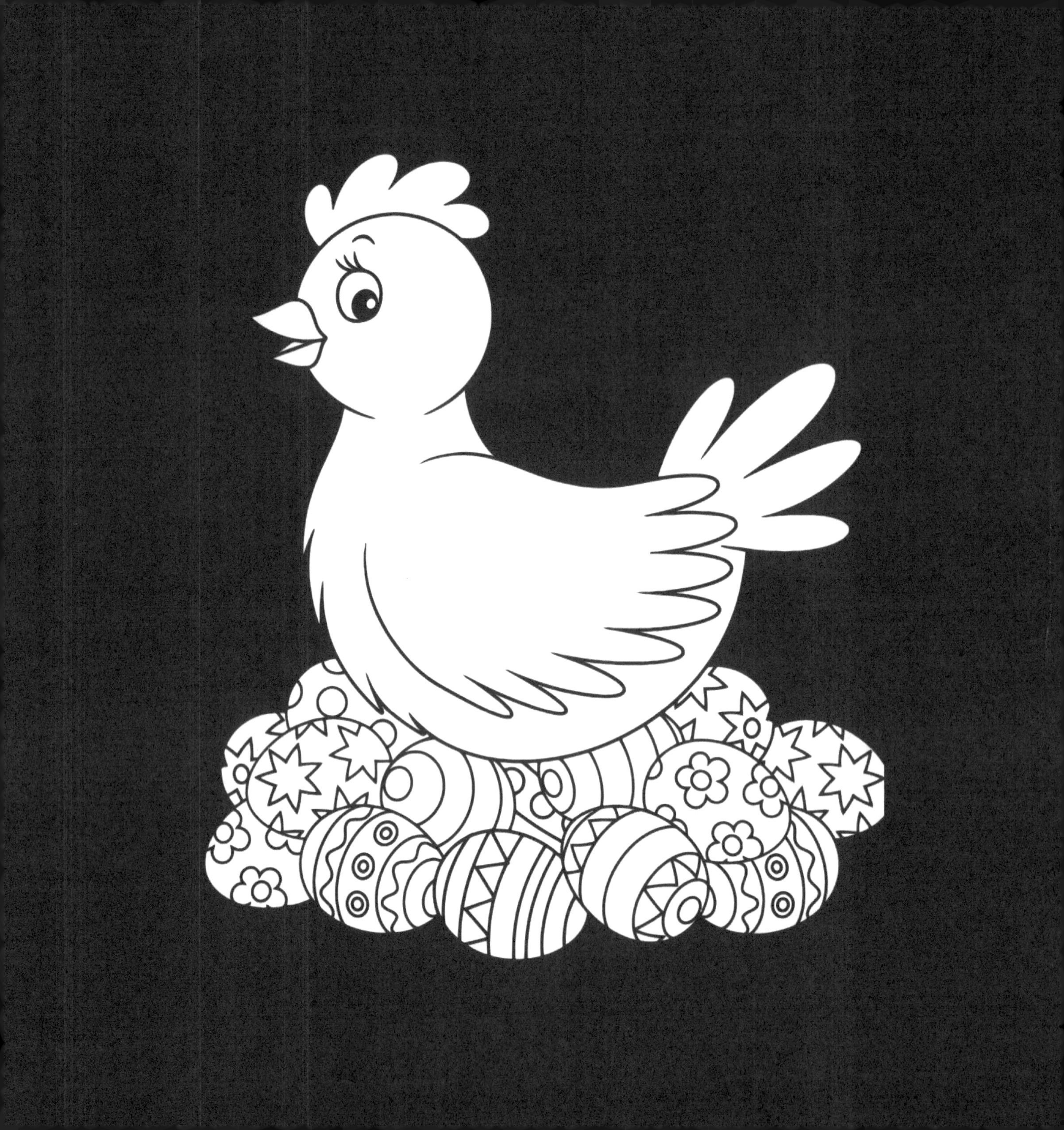

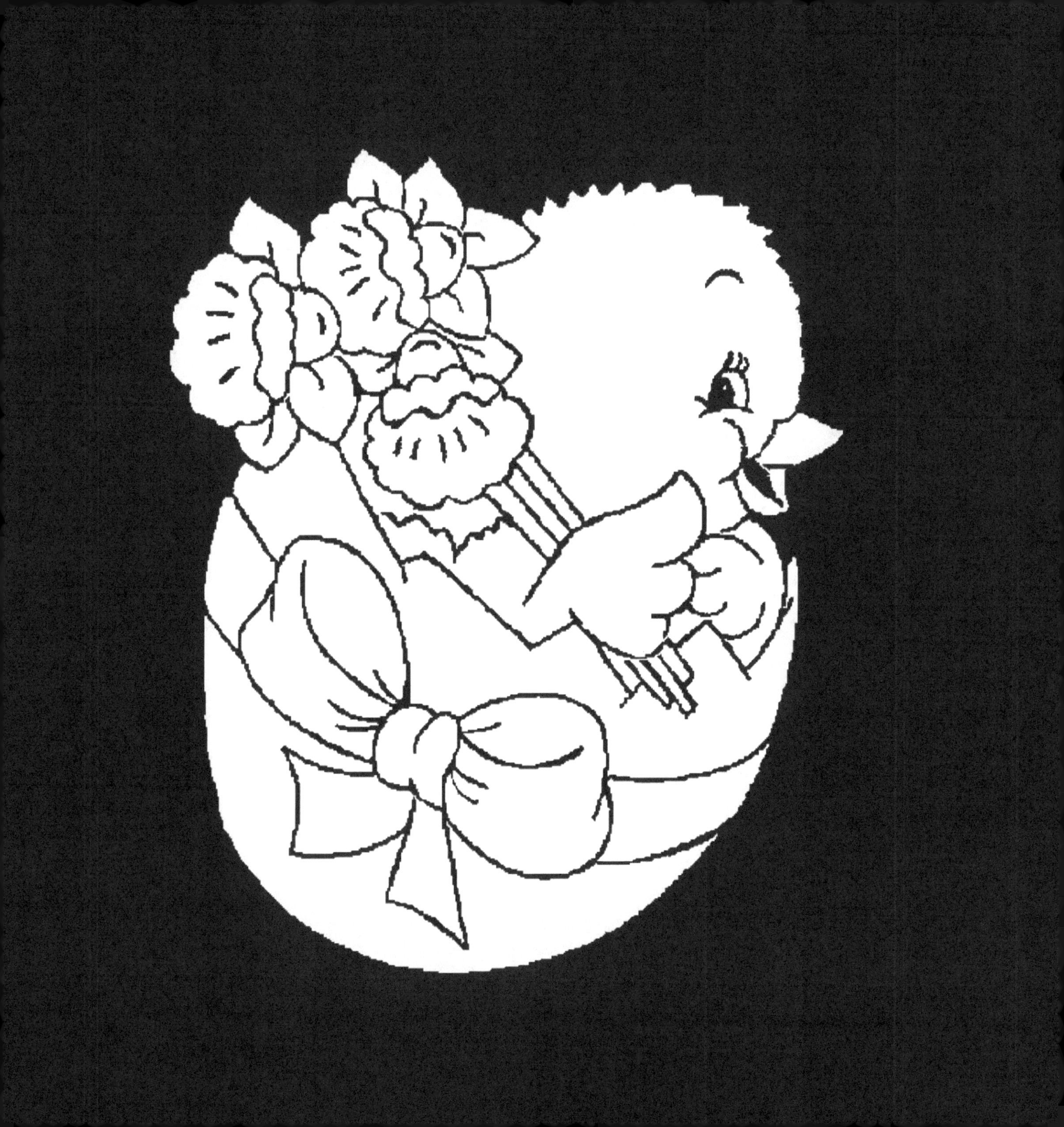

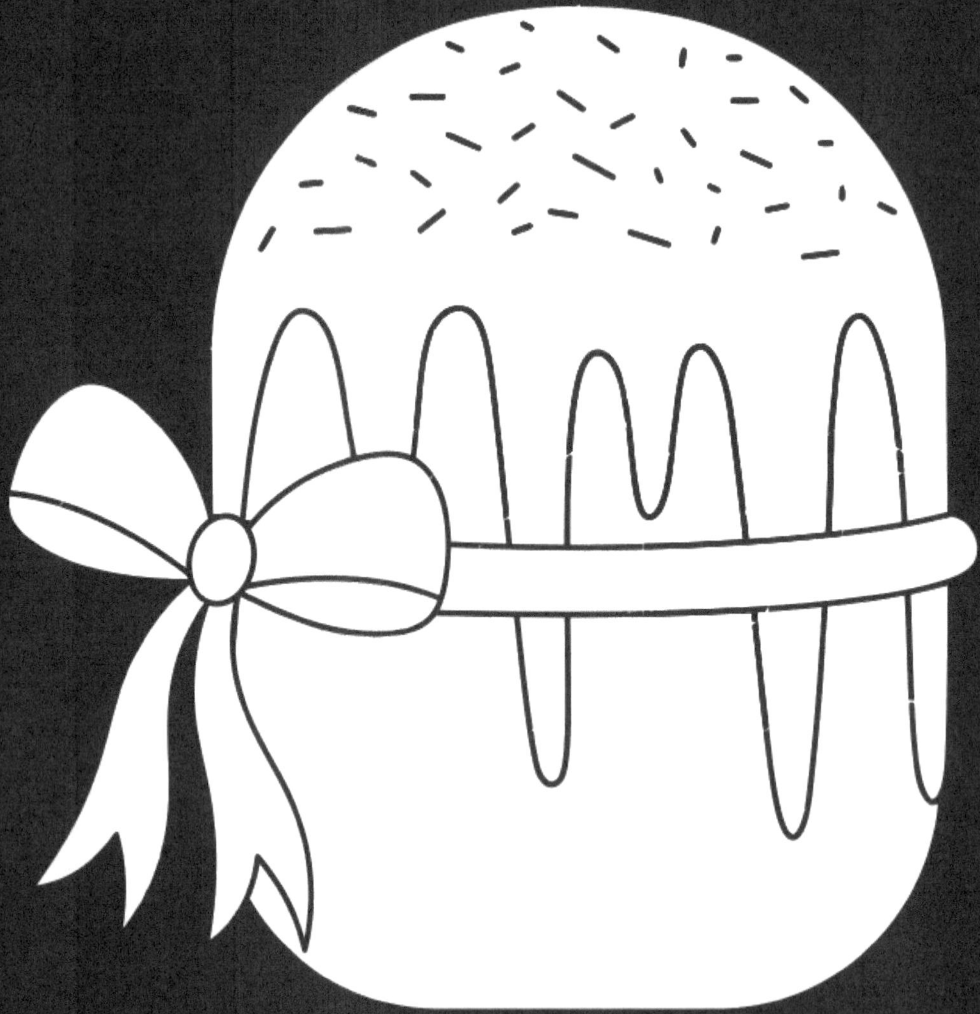

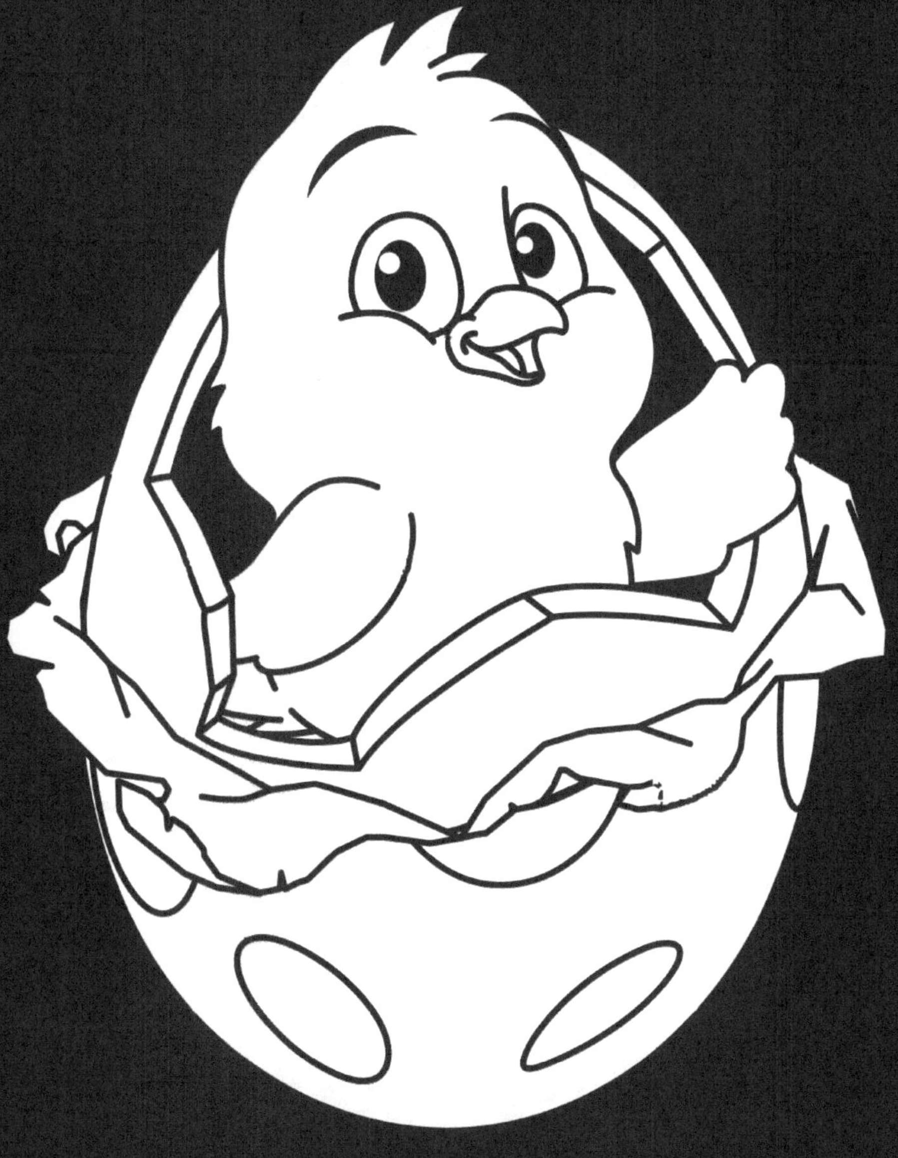

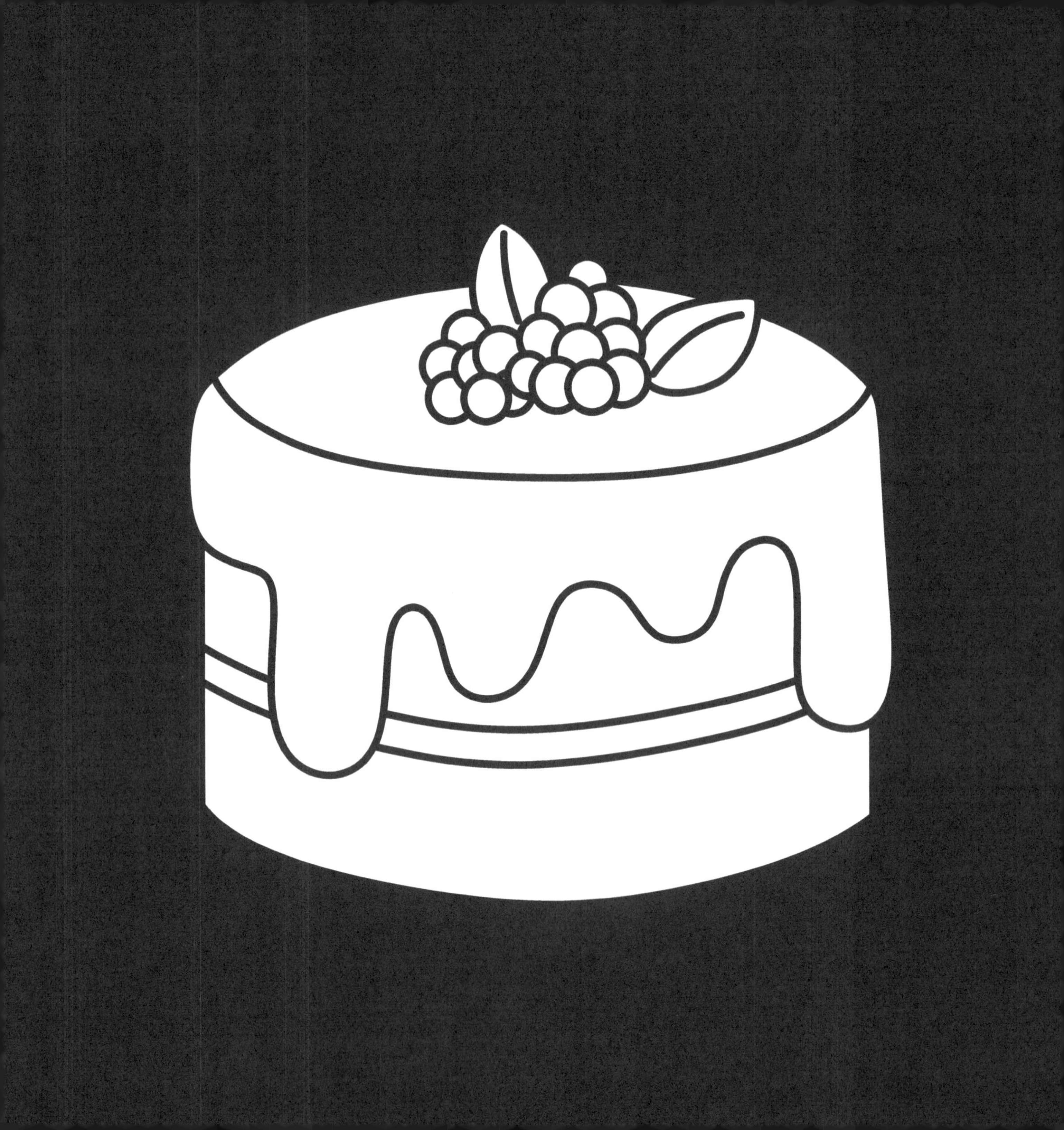

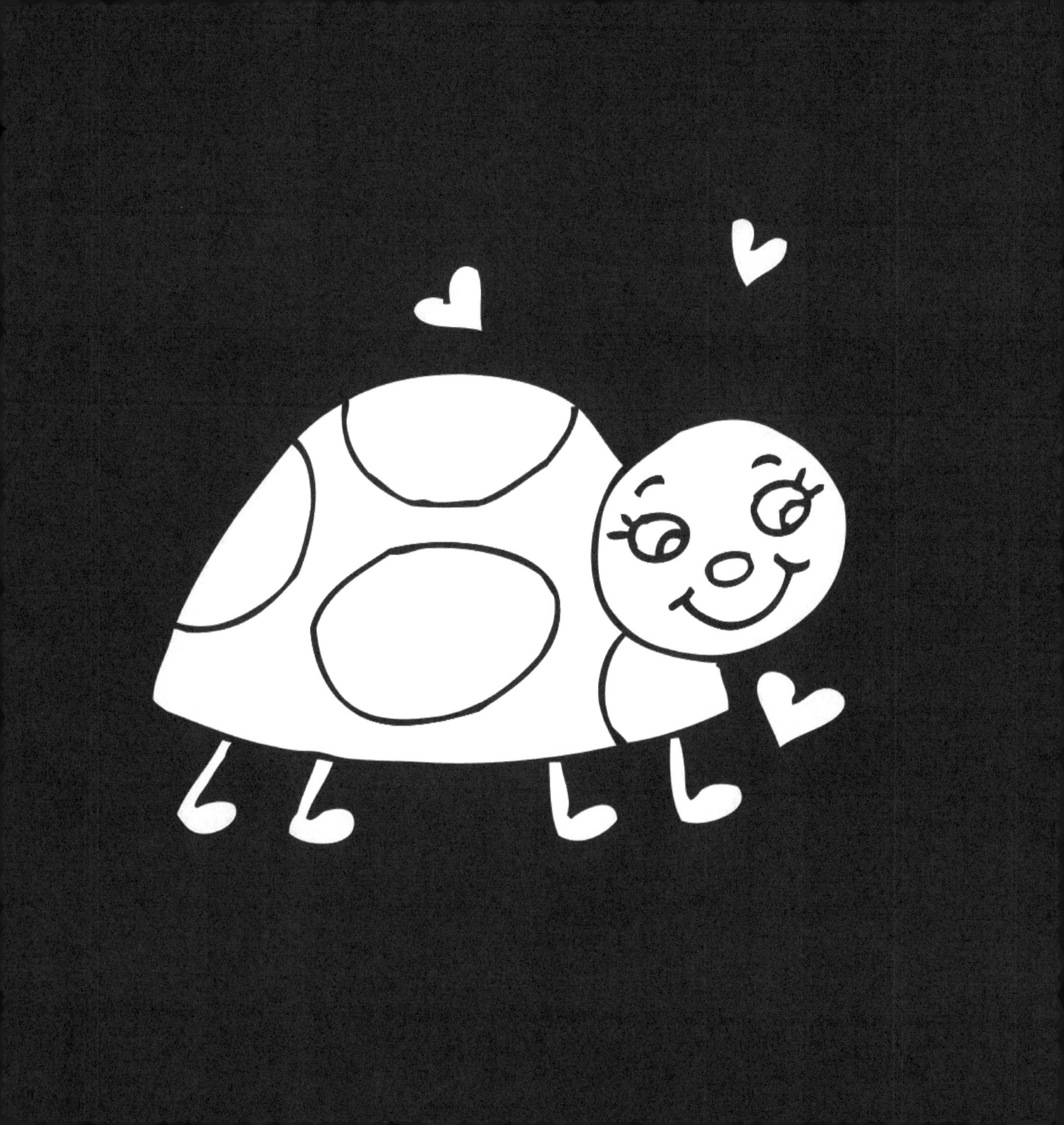

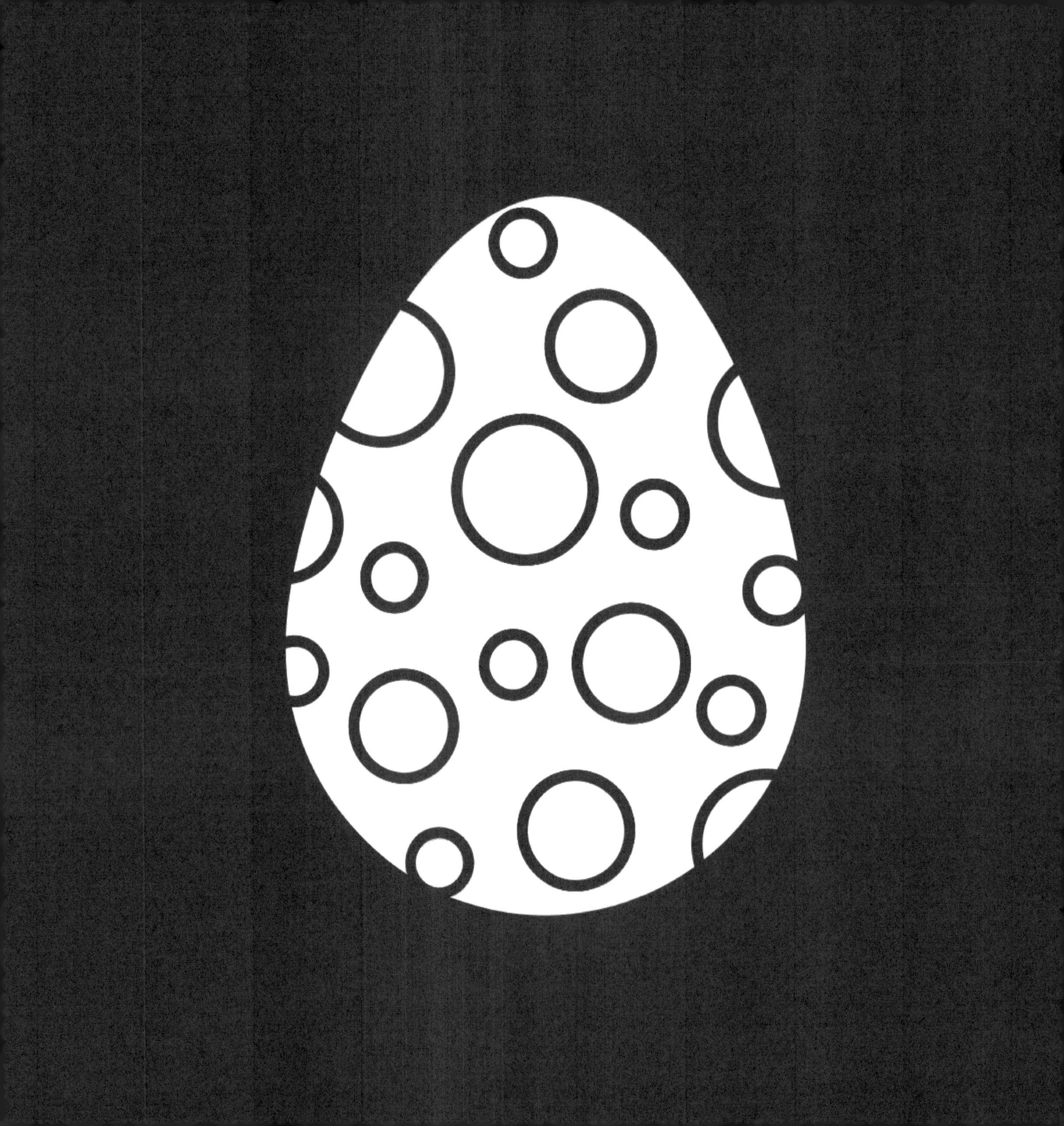

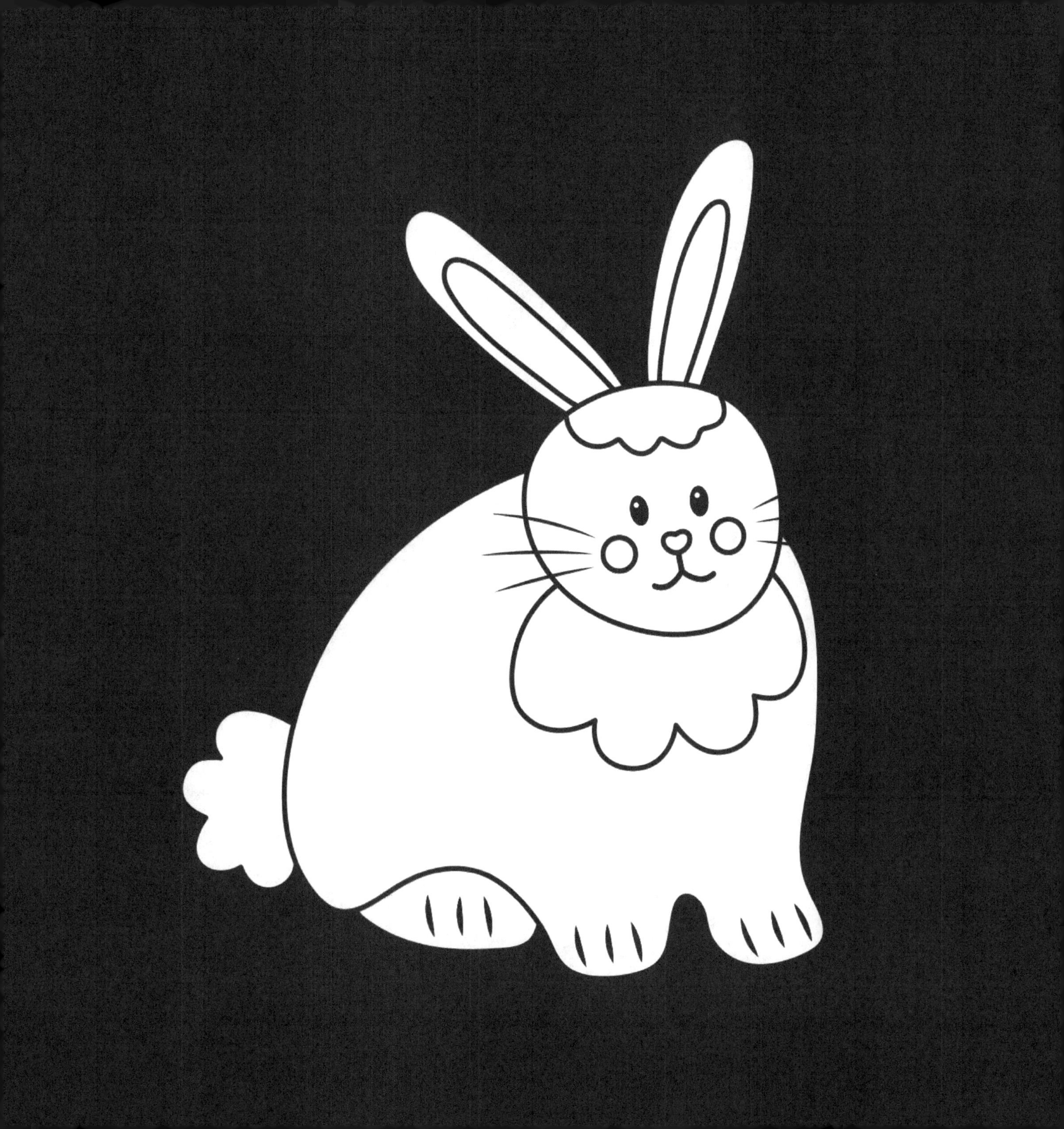

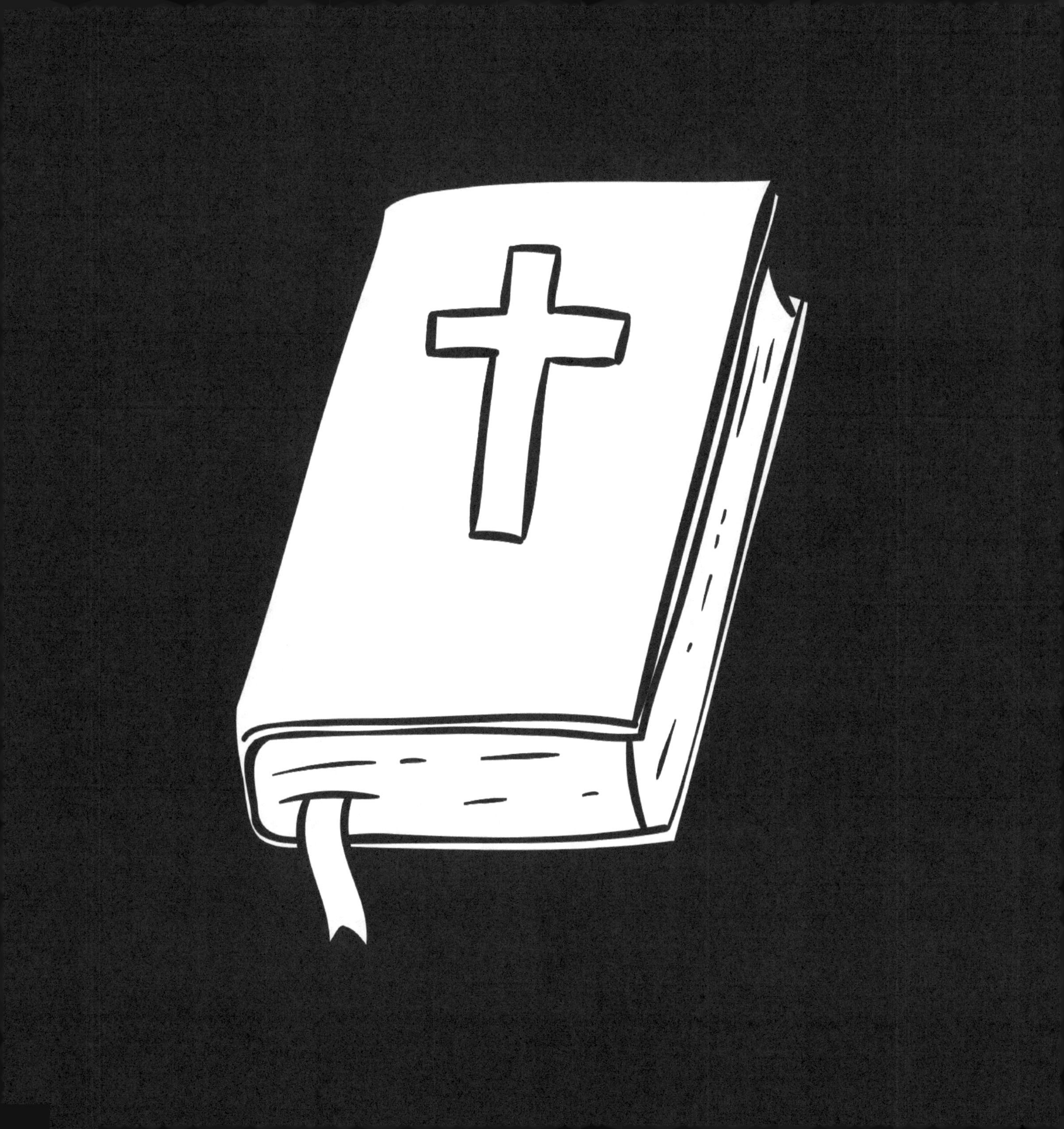

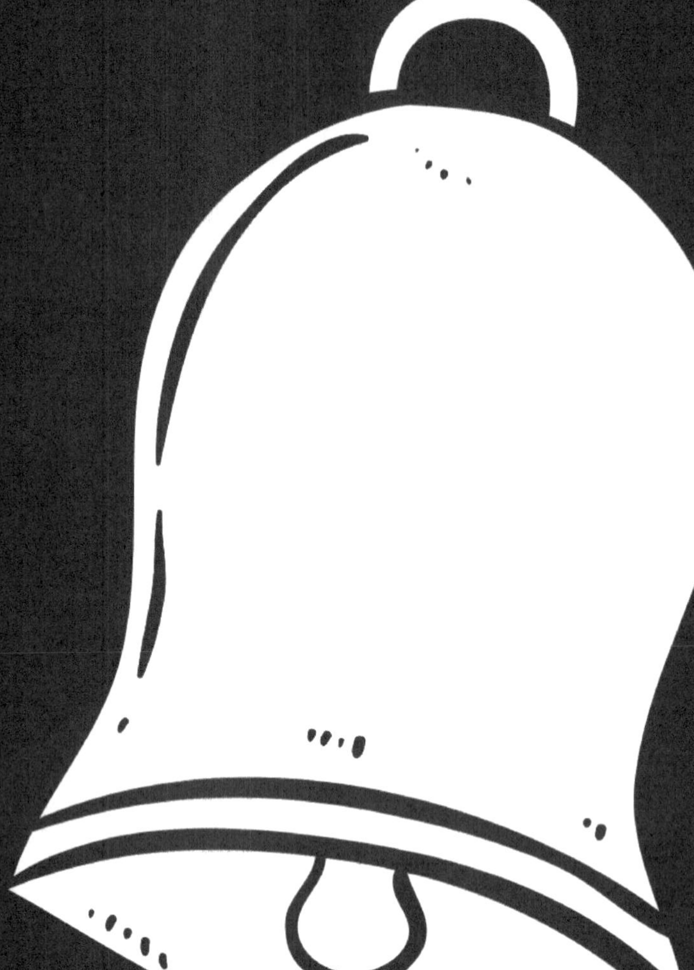

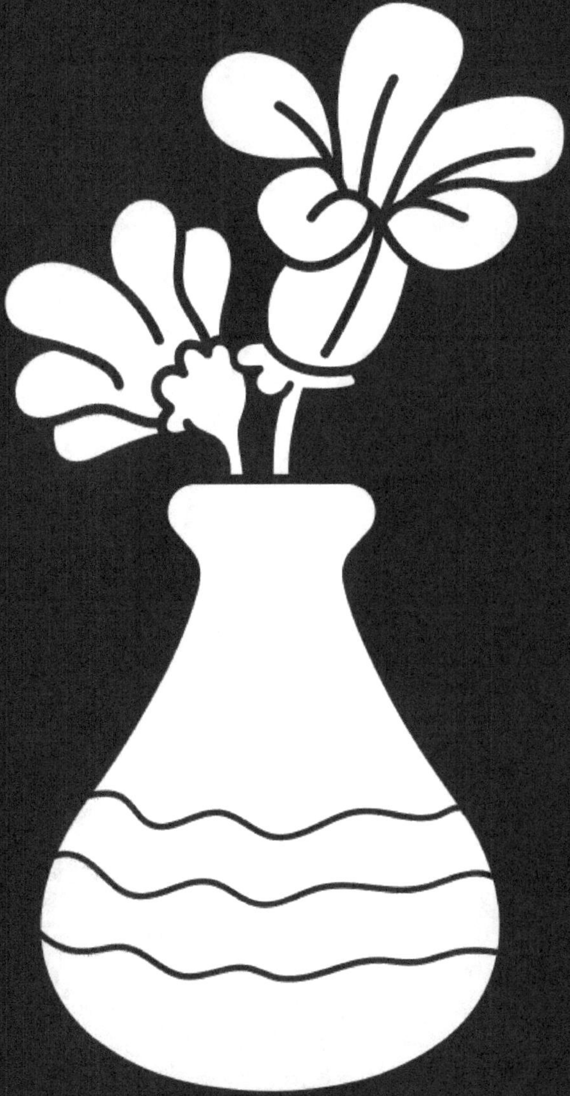

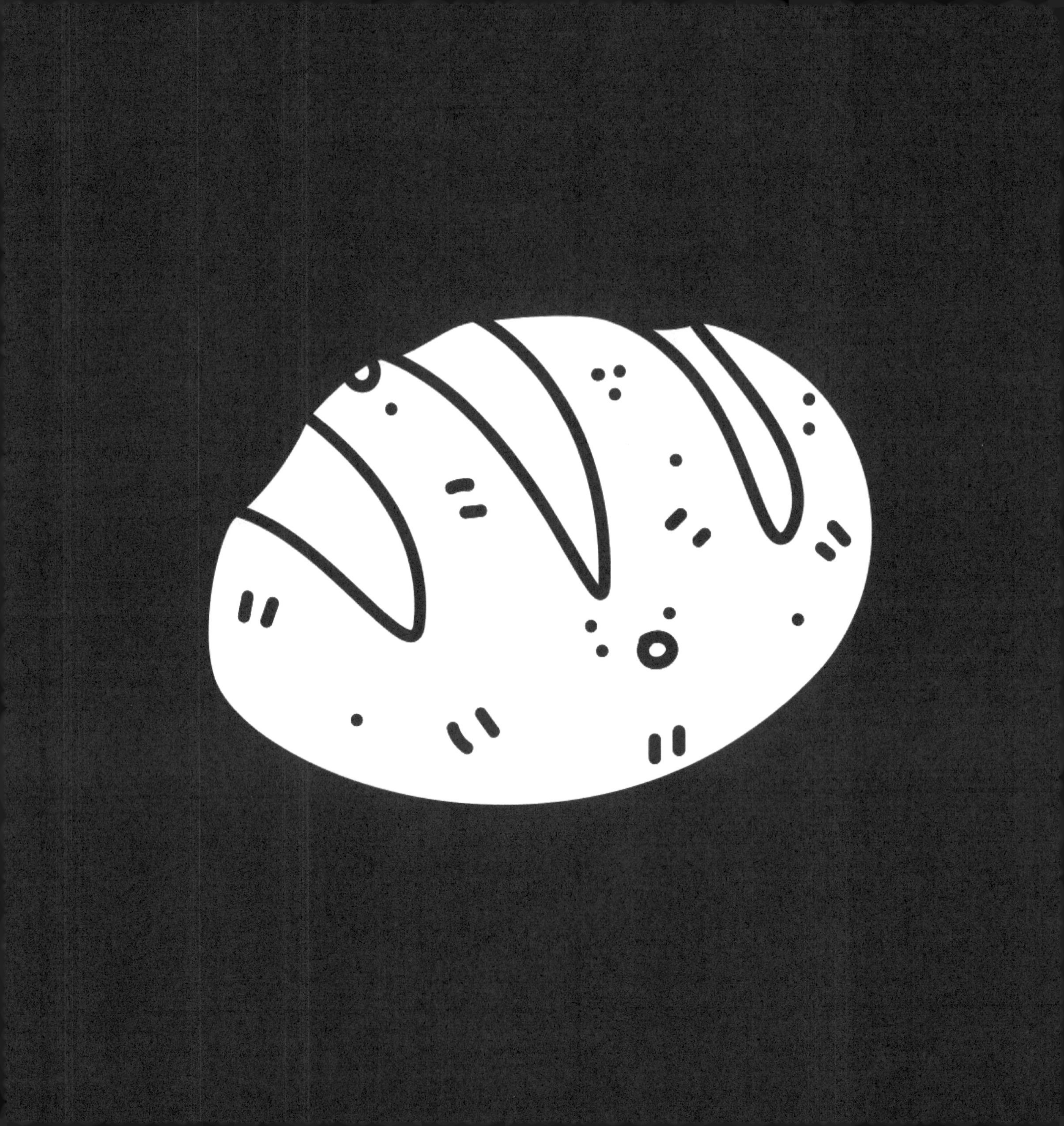

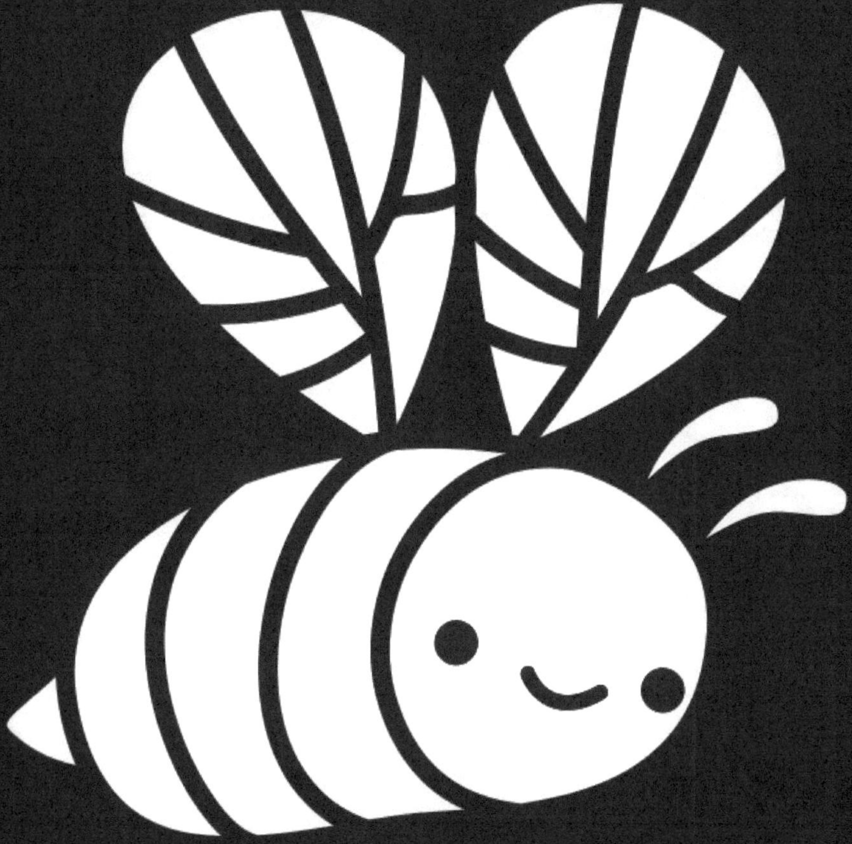

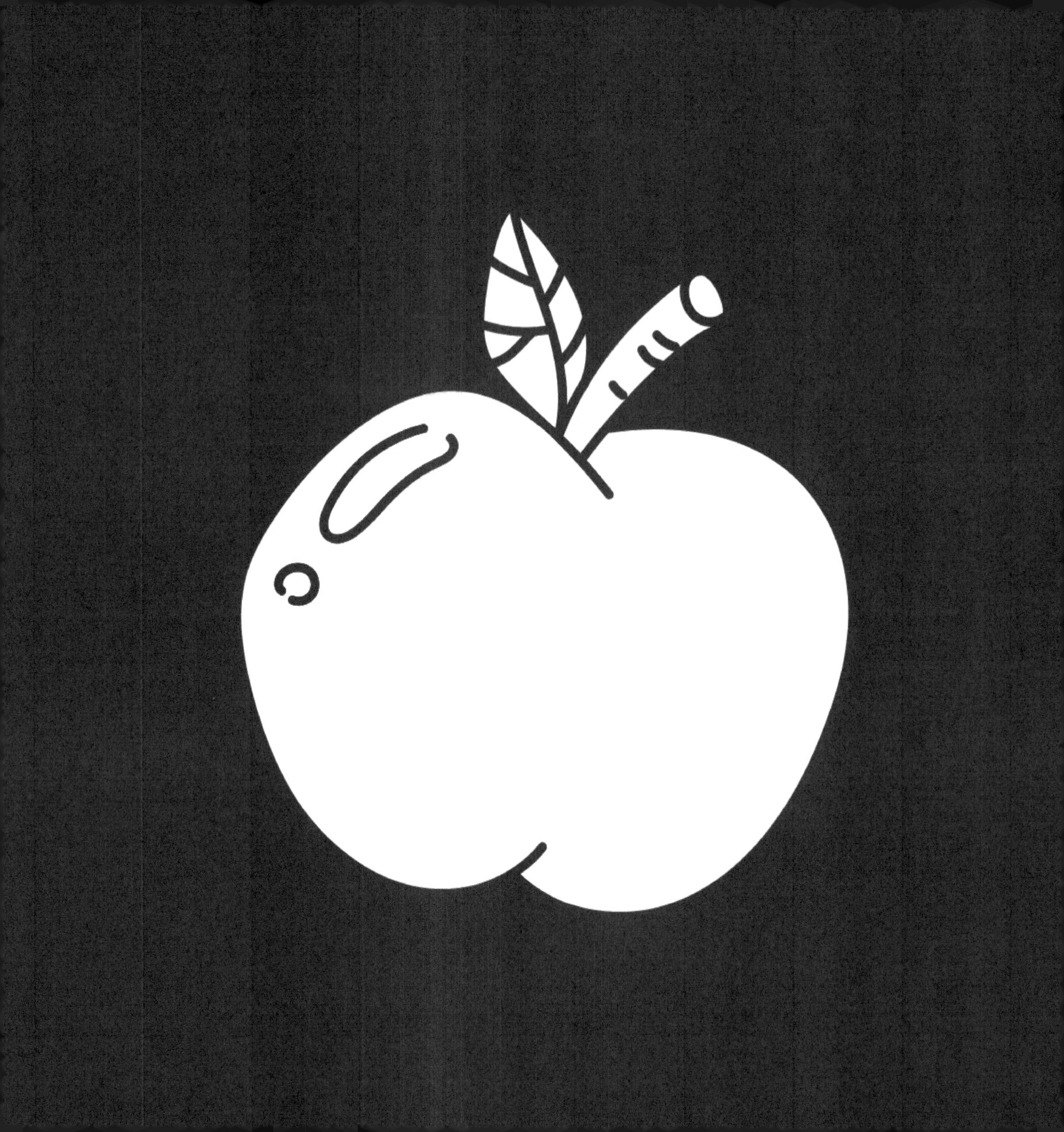

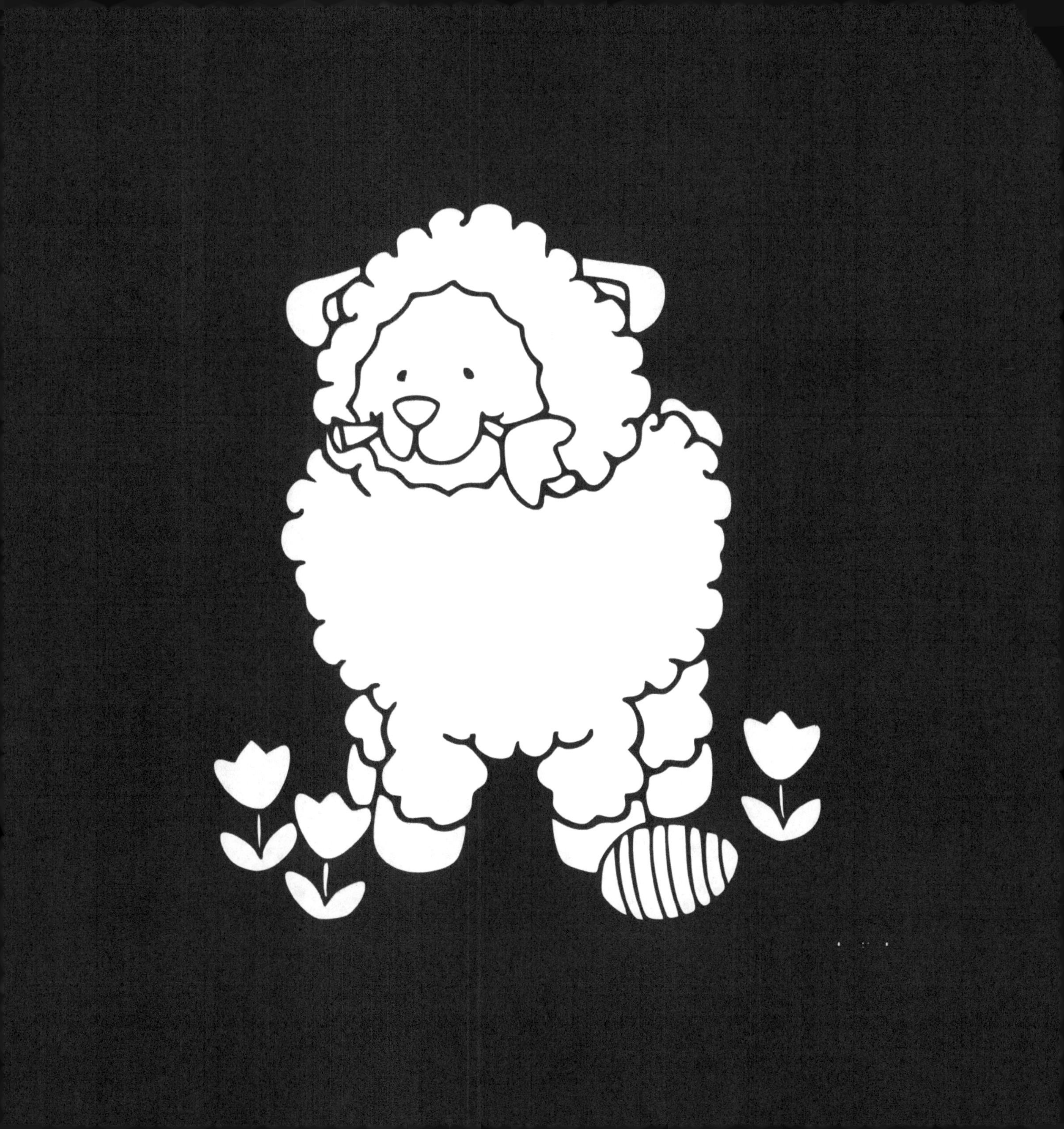

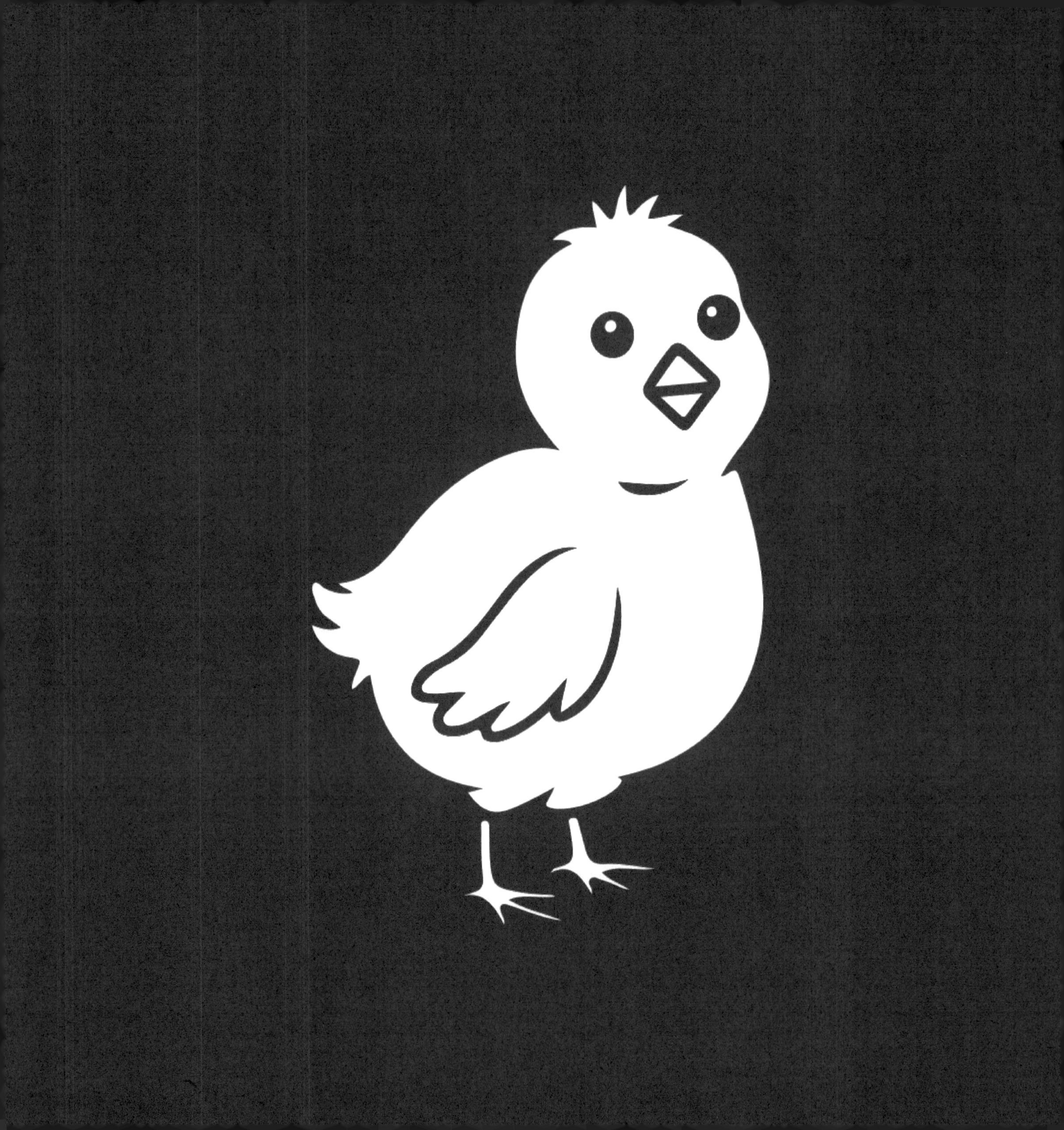

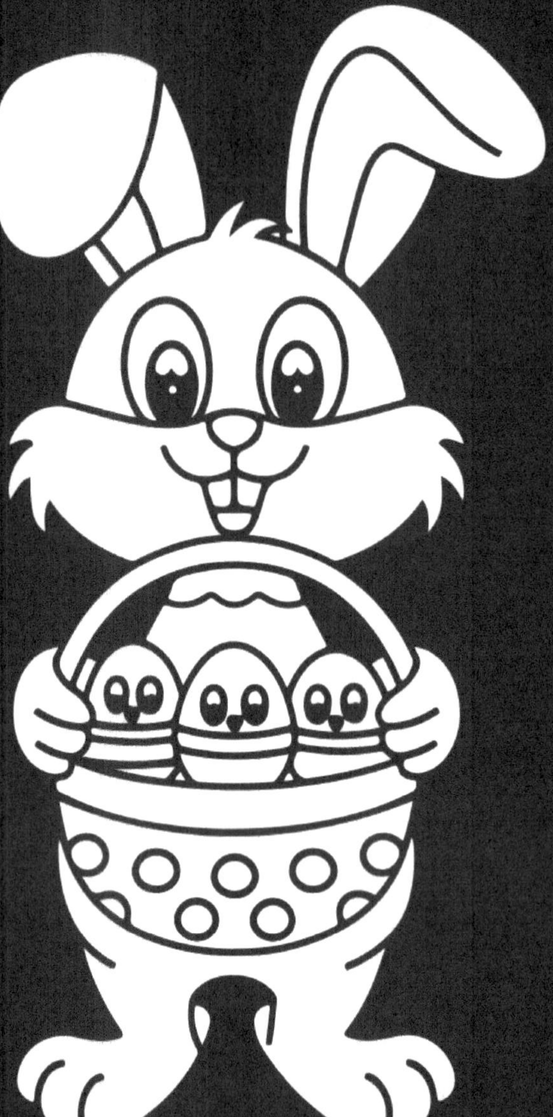

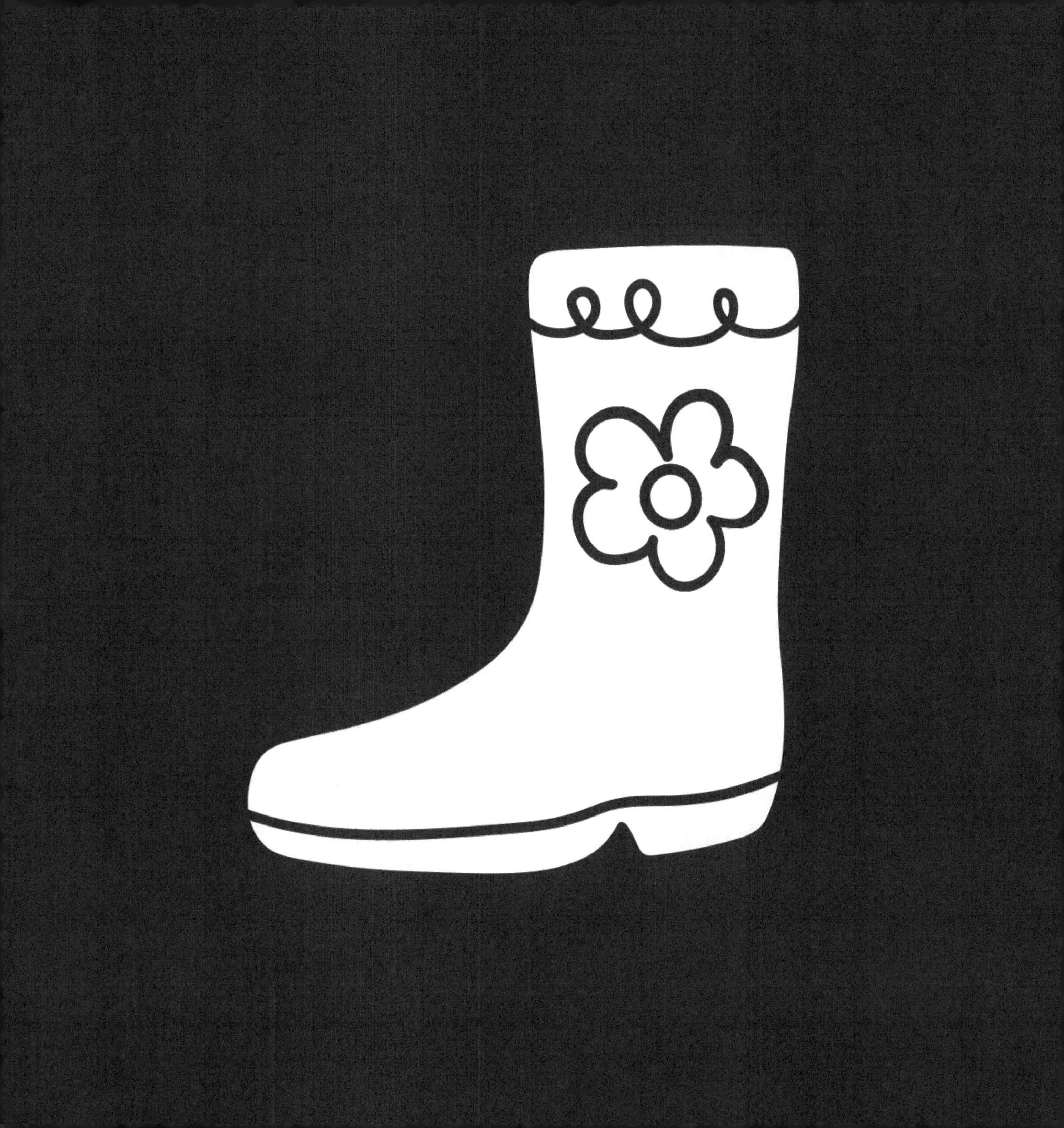

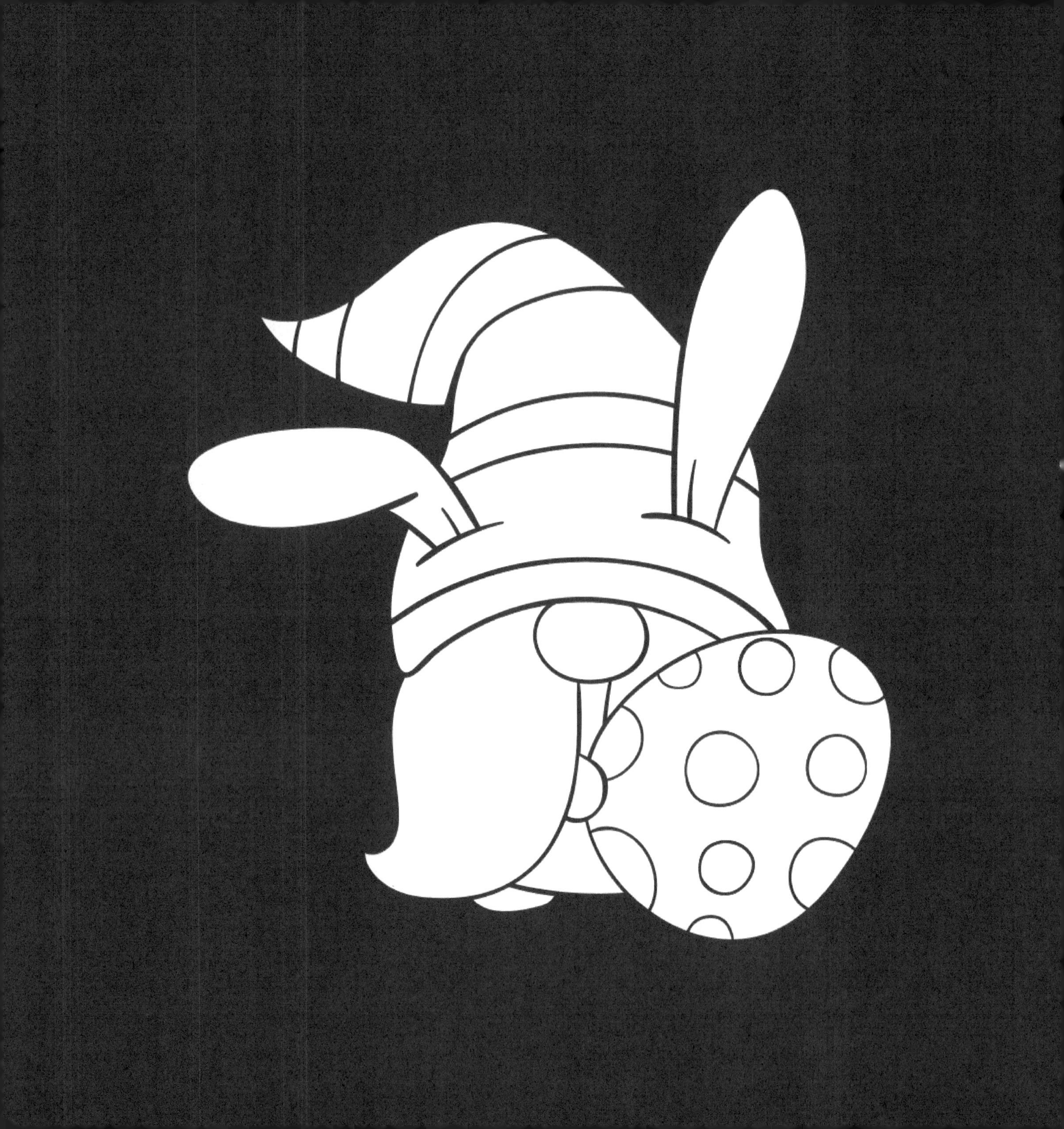

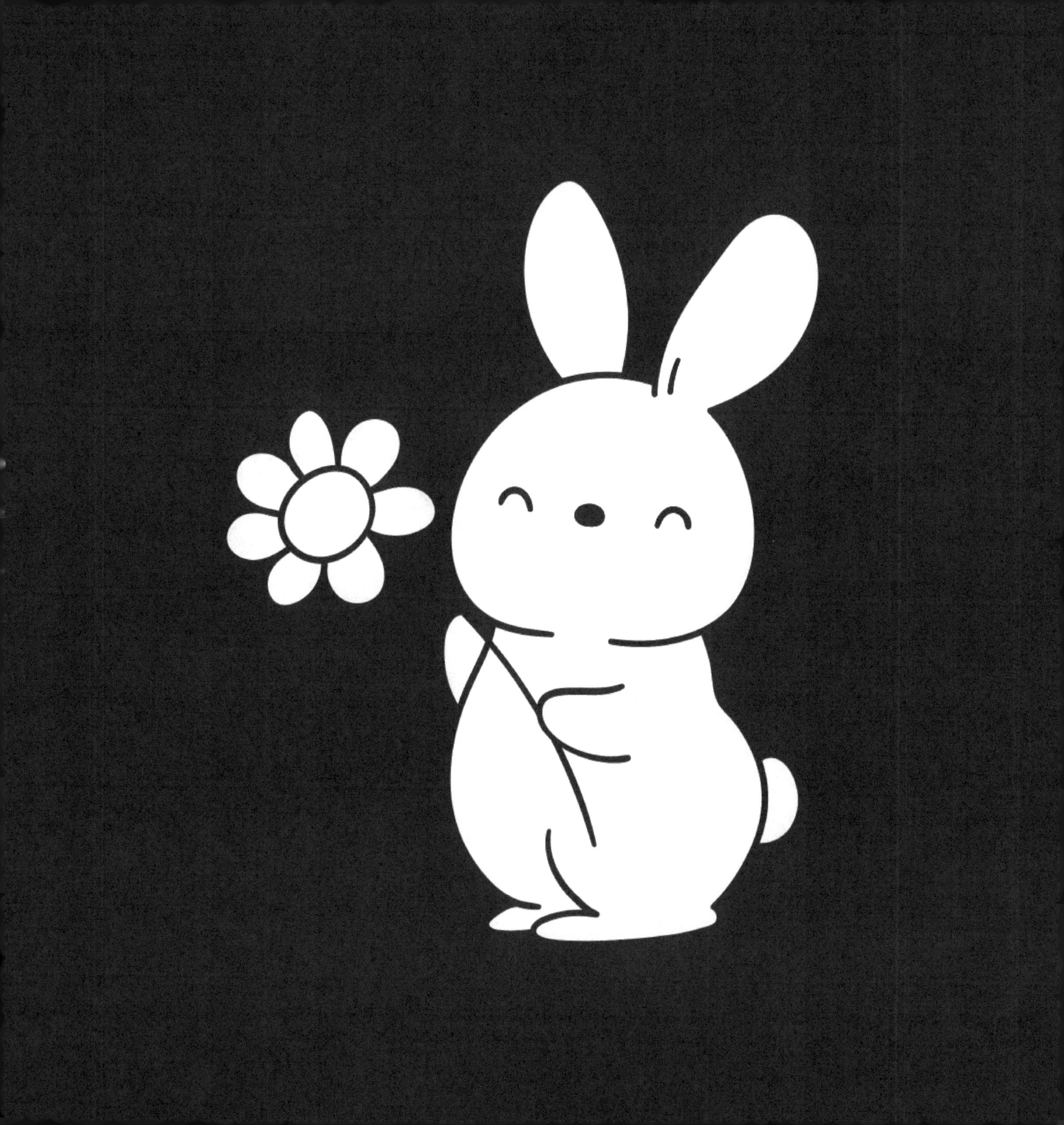

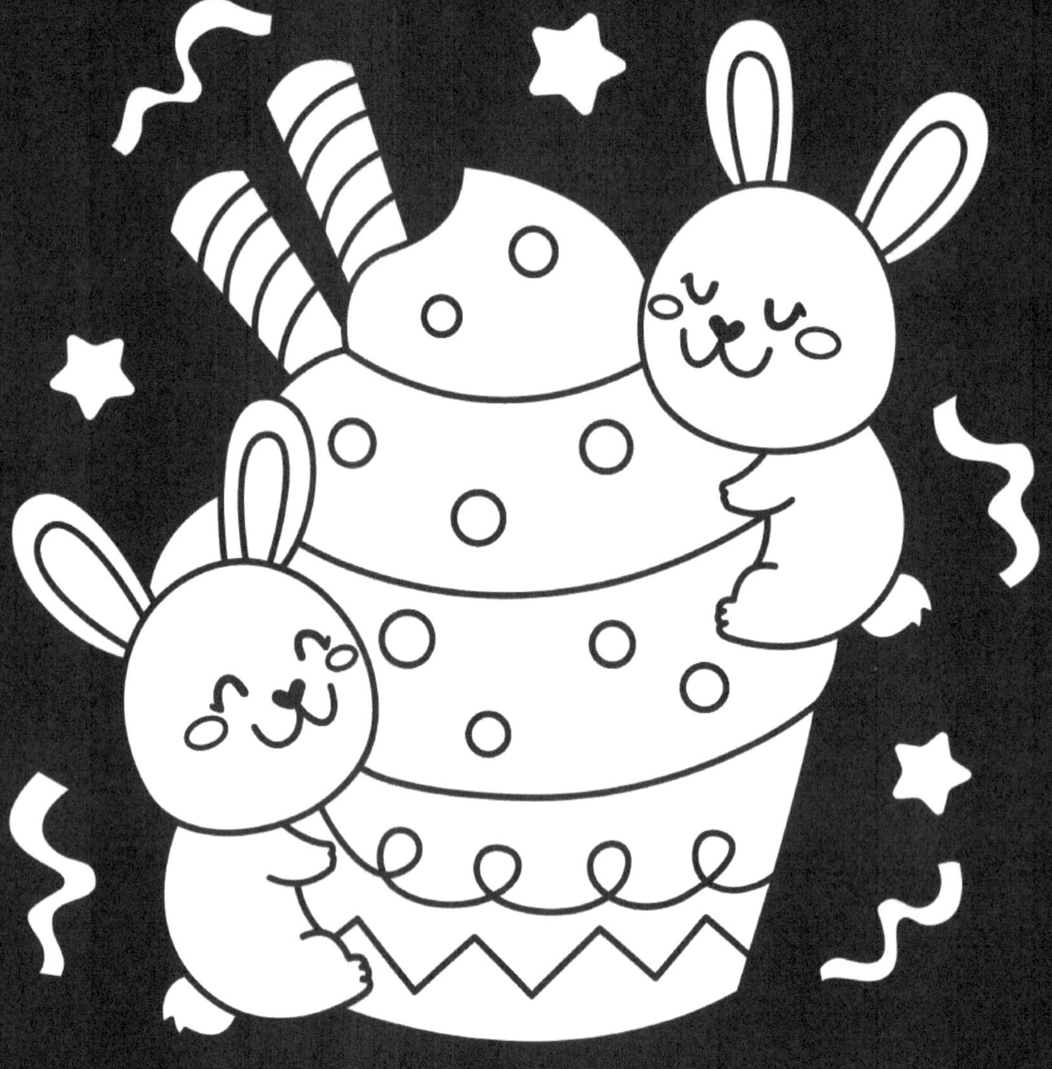

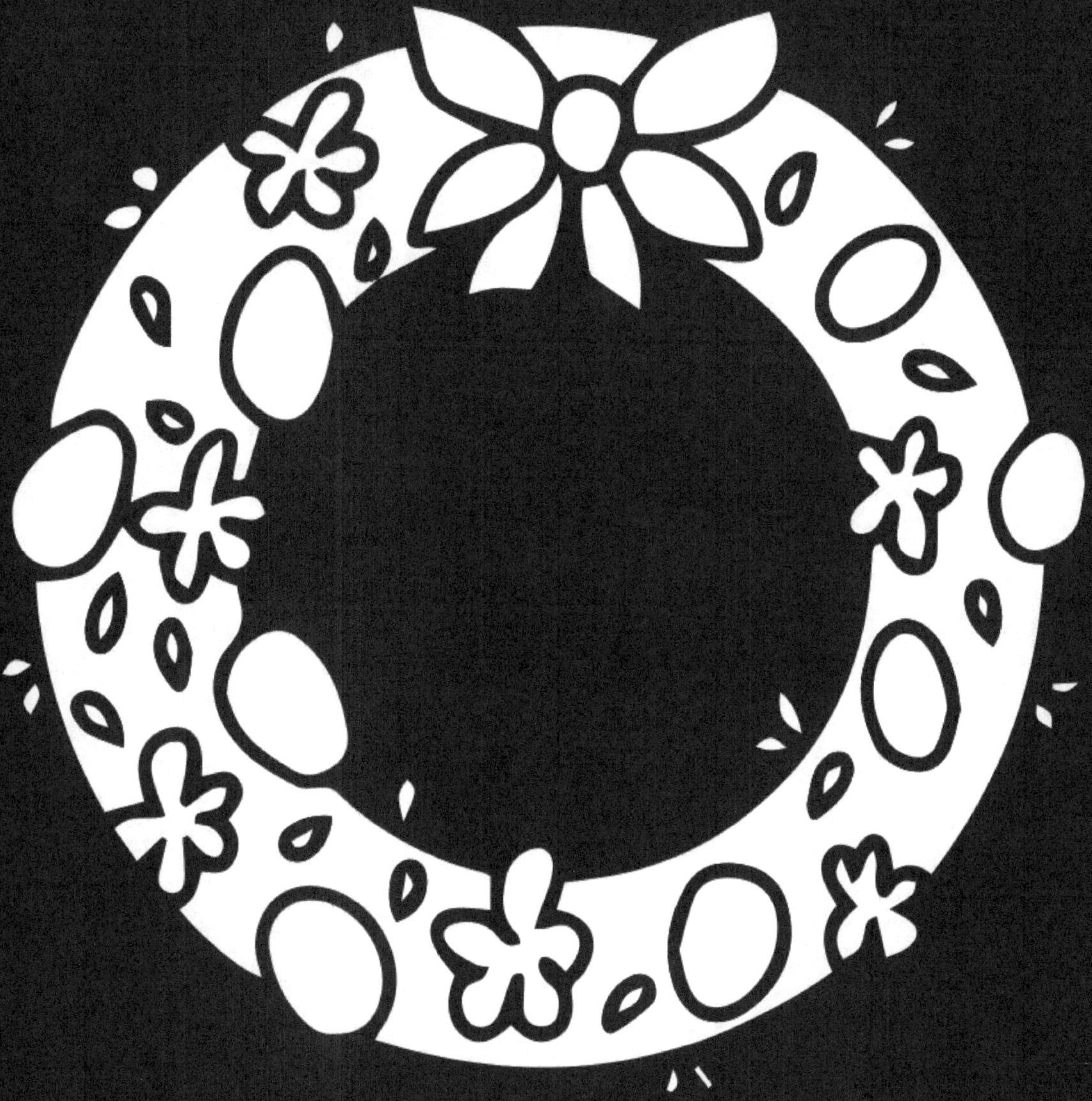

Happy Easter

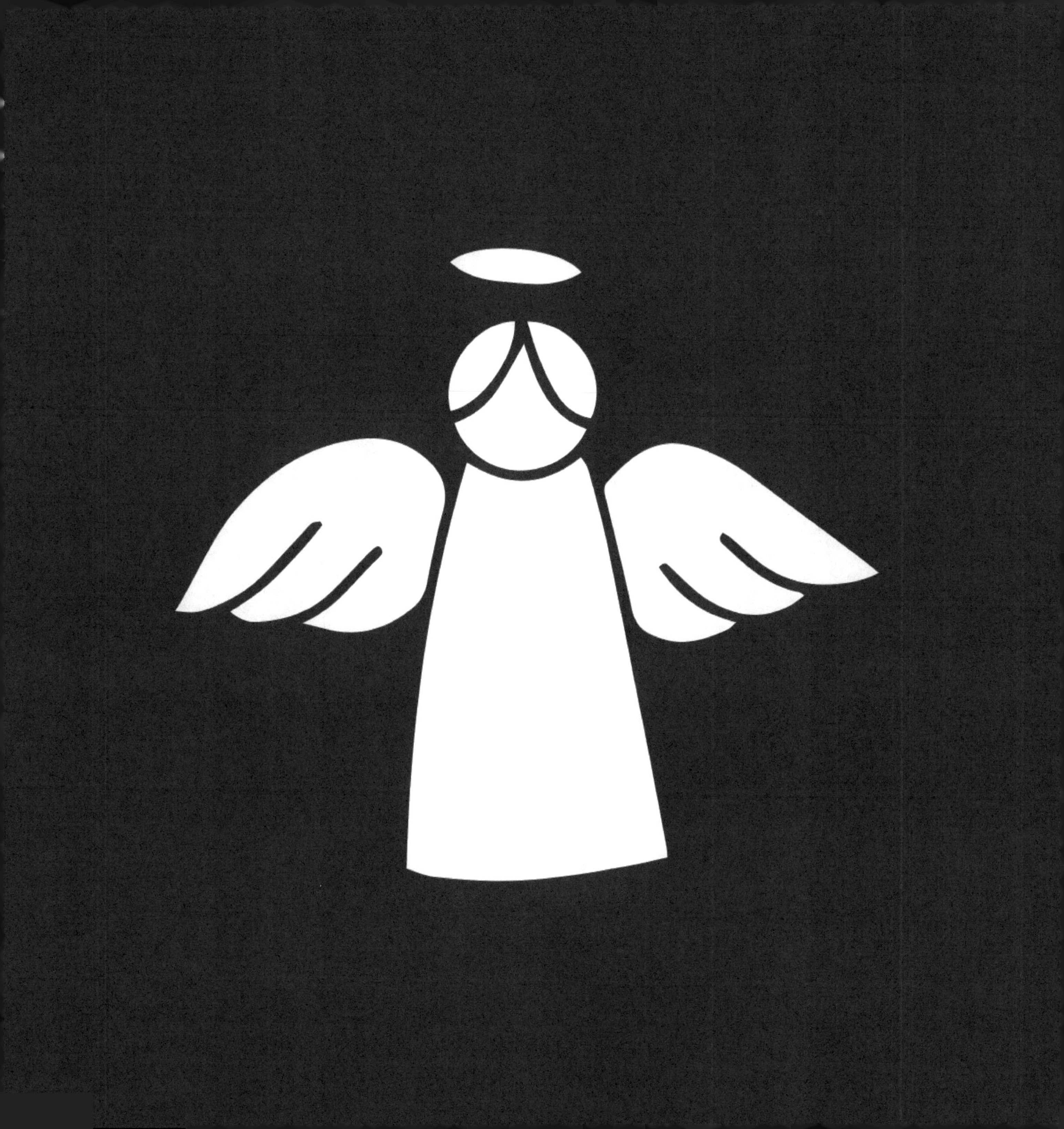

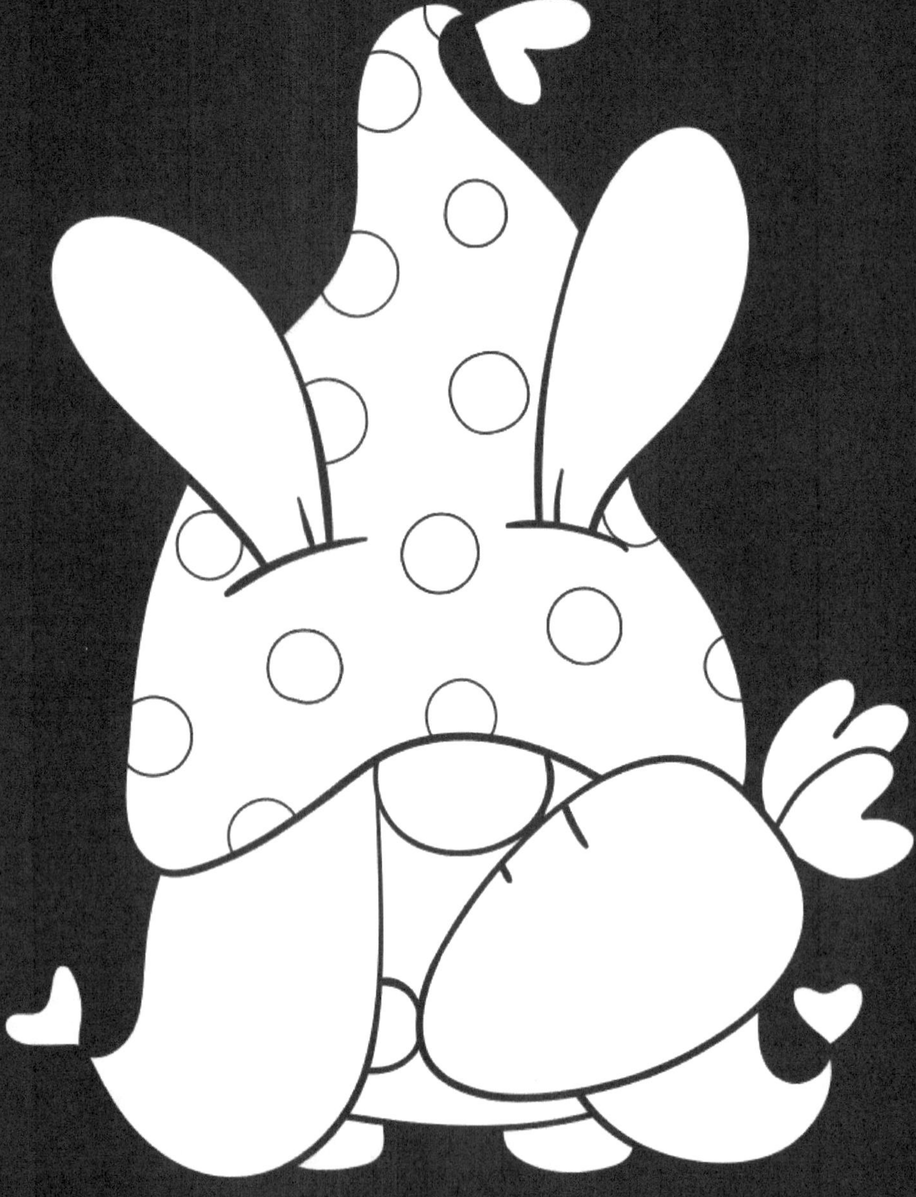